ENLIGHTENED EQUITATION

ENLIGHTENED EQUITATION

RIDING IN TRUE HARMONY WITH YOUR HORSE

Heather Moffett

David & Charles

**To my father and late mother, without whose help
this book would never have been possible**

Line artwork by DIANNE BREEZE except pp32, 33 and 37 by
    Maggie Raynor

All photographs by IAIN BURNS except the following:
pp2, 7, 72, 73, 74, 87, 148–9, and front and back cover photographs,
    Your Horse magazine
pp12, 13, 39, 46, 51, 91, 106, 123, 130, 143, 144, 145, 146–7 from
    author's collection
p15, 142 Bob Langrish
p28 Photo by Authenticolor, Geneva, used by kind permission of
    Miss Silvia Stanier LVO
p71 Kit Houghton
p104 Gilsons Photography
p105 Anthony E. Reynolds LBIPP LMPA
p151 Joanna Prestwich
p154 *Horse* magazine

A DAVID & CHARLES BOOK

First published in the UK in 1999
Reprinted 2000, 2001

Text Copyright © Heather Moffett 1999

Heather Moffett has asserted her right to be identified as author of this work in
accordance with the Copyright, Designs and Patents Act, 1988.

A catalogue record for this book is available from the British Library.

ISBN 0 7153 0810 6

Book designed by Visual Image
Printed and bound in Great Britain
by Butler & Tanner Limited, Frome and London
for David & Charles
Brunel House   Newton Abbot   Devon

CONTENTS

INTRODUCTION

Read any of the 'question-and-answer' features in today's equestrian magazines, and the chances are that you will find several queries devoted to resistances and evasions. 'My horse will not go forward', 'My horse bucks', 'My horse rears' and others in a similar vein are all too common a subject for the equine 'agony aunts'.

While several well-known horsemen and women are currently doing sterling work to bring to the attention of the equestrian public the fact that the horse not only has feelings, but also possesses its own special communication system which we can tune into, and are solving many of the handling and behavioural problems on the ground, I believe that they are addressing only part of the problem. Having spent a lifetime with horses, and the last 26 years as a teacher of riding, I have – through a long study of the interaction between horse and rider – become firmly convinced that **in probably 75 per cent of cases the relationship breaks down under saddle first, due to poor riding techniques**.

I do not believe that conventional methods of handling and breaking the young horse are to blame. In general, lungeing, long-reining and so on are not traumatic for the horse, and help to prepare him for the time when he will be asked to carry a rider. It is once the horse is ridden that the problems begin to creep in because the rider is, often inadvertently, giving the horse rough and confusing signals, and is frequently impeding him by incorrect interaction with his movement. Through discomfort, the horse starts to misbehave, and in turn the rider becomes apprehensive. The horse then senses this fear and plays up all the more, not necessarily through a desire to get the better of the rider, but often through lack of confidence in the person to whom he would normally look for guidance as his leader, but from whom he is receiving no feedback.

I have seen it happen more times than I care to remember. The owner now no longer enjoys riding the horse, who is 'misbehaving', and may eventually reach the point of not wanting to ride him at all. Still paying out for his keep and turning out in all weather to look after a horse that 'cannot be ridden', even though it is perfectly fit and sound, quickly adds up to bitterness and resentment on the part of the owner. Often the horse is difficult to sell on because it has developed behavioural problems so the owner, stuck with the situation, gradually bothers less and less about the horse's welfare.

Some years ago, disillusioned with the mainstream methods of teaching and training, I began to experiment with variations on the way in which the rider absorbs the horse's movement in order to stay on, and some interesting findings came to light. My own method of teaching shows riders how to mirror closely the movements of the horse's back with their own, but during my research it soon became clear to me that **some of the more common riding techniques actually impede the horse's forward movement, and yet these are routinely taught in riding schools**. As a result, the rider is being actively encouraged to prevent the horse's ability to work, resulting in the need to use more leg, more whip, more spur. The horse, resenting the punishment that he does not deserve, or even comprehend, starts to rebel, and so the rot sets in. **Few horses are truly born bad – they are made difficult by human hands**.

Instead, if riders are taught from day one the correct biomechanical interaction between horse and rider, and to learn to listen to the horse, all of these problems can be avoided. The methods of 'Enlightened Equitation' are simple, logical, and mostly based on tried and tested Classical techniques. The rider must have a clear understanding of the 'nuts and bolts' of riding if the horse is not to become confused. This book provides that information, for beginners and novices, for experienced riders with established faults who wish to improve, and for instructors who wish to gain a broader understanding in order to teach a better way to ride, where **partnership, not domination, is the only goal**.

Heather riding Doric. Doric, sadly no longer with us, acted as a wonderful demonstration model for a photography session for *Your Horse* magazine (*by kind permission of Suzanne's Riding School, Harrow*)

Left: Sue Beck riding her Andalucian x Trakehner mare, Flame. I had only worked with the mare once before, and thought (having seen her bucking and leaping around on the lunge) that she was a real fireball. In fact she is very idle and backward-thinking, not at all what you would expect from her breeding. She is stunningly beautiful, but Sue hasn't had a straightforward task at all, and makes her look much easier than she really is!

Centre: Jo White and Max, a homebred Warmblood who had continually suffered with problems which had mostly been attributed to the back area. Well known 'back man' Tex Gamble isolated the source of the trouble: a one-inch splinter of bone in Max's mouth. The pain had

Left: Debbie Survila on Woody. Woody is Irish Draught x TB, and one of my favourite horses to ride. He is wonderfully light for such a hefty chap, responsive to the lightest aid, and in fact you can school him for an hour and hardly feel as if you have ridden. He is learning all his lateral work with ease, and will be a great demonstration horse, showing that you don't need to have an expensive foreign Warmblood to do dressage.

Centre: Stephanie Garcia-Olmo on Corpus. Corpus is a 9-year-old ex-racehorse, now being reschooled for eventing. As readers will see by the photographs accompanying his case history on pages 110–17 he is an enormously talented horse with a great attitude to his work.

been causing him to draw back from the contact and contort his neck and back. The bone duly removed, he is now a different horse

Right: Donna Wyatt and Juniper, a purebred Lipizzaner. She is a wonderfully responsive forward-going ride, who will find piaffe and passage easy. She is only 14.2hh, but is one of the widest horses I have ever sat on! When fitting her for a saddle, I faxed the template to my saddler who asked if I had made a mistake, saying it was the widest saddle he had ever made in over twenty years in the trade. Donna is quite little, so she does well to sit so well when she's nearly doing the splits!

Right: Debbie Mumford and Beenleighford Moonraker, Champion Connemara pony. Debbie had owned Moon since a foal, sold him at 4 years old, and bought him back just over a year later! He has not been an easy pony to train, being extremely fussy in the mouth. He is now a winner and champion of breed classes, and is continuing his dressage training. He is only 14hh, but his movement is as big and powerful to sit as many Warmbloods half as big again.

HEATHER'S METHODS WORK...

Far too few people seem to realise the effect their bodies and their riding have on their horses. Because the rider feels fairly comfortable, he or she assumes that the horse is OK, but I am sure that this is often far from the case.

Horses, like people, react differently in response to discomfort or pain. Many horses are stoical and simply put up with it; others respond actively and become 'difficult', even dangerous, ending up being branded as 'problem horses'. Imagine how confusing conflicting, ambiguous messages must be to an animal as sensitive as the horse, and how much intelligence and reasoning power must be needed on his part to try to sort them out and decide what the rider actually wants him to do.

Heather has developed a simple, logical method of equitation which, if applied correctly and with consideration for the horse, can do away with all the confusion and make for happier, more confident and secure horses, and also give riders a greater sense of achievement and harmony with their horses. We both had instruction from the same teacher of Classical equitation, Desi Lorent, and I can not only understand where her system is coming from, but also appreciate the extensions she has made to it. Heather does not like being called a 'Classical' teacher because the term has been misused in recent years, not least because a lot of teachers under the Classical banner do not, in fact, teach Classical principles. She uses the term 'Enlightened Equitation', appropriate because you do have to think of horses in a more sensitive and empathetic way than is often taught today to understand and feel the philosophy of her system.

Having watched many individual exponents of 'Classical' equitation, it has to be said that sometimes their horses don't look entirely happy! Not infrequently you cannot fail to see, or even just sense, an air of constraint about them, however slight. The horse often seems to be saying that although he is *reasonably* relaxed and comfortable he would rather have a little more freedom to give his insightful version of what he is being asked for.

You do not see this with Heather's horses, or those ridden by people correctly applying her principles. The horses all seem quite comfortable, confidently enjoying the movements they're performing, thinking about what might be wanted next, swinging along correctly and freely and having as good a time as their riders. Above all, there is no constraint, anxiety or tension. To me, this is what harmonious equitation is all about. Her methods work with 'difficult' horses, too, not least because their difficulties have often been caused by bad riding practice in the past, and the horses now expect to have problems, acting by habit before the event.

Having bought an old Thoroughbred mare who could pull like a train and take off with her riders (even in trot) when the mood took her, and who knew every human and equine trick in the book, I found myself totally unwilling and unable to use the traditional and harsh techniques often recommended, and knew they would not work on a horse with her temperament.

I turned to Heather for advice. The trick? The gist of it was, before any increase in gait, to make sure I had her softly flexed to the bit by means of a half-moon pelham used mainly and gently on the curb rein (which the mare preferred to any other bit and technique) and she would remain balanced, controlled and usually calm. Although her temperament caused her to hot up sometimes, I ended up with a wonderful, exhilarating hack who never again pulled hard or went faster than I wanted, and most of the time was happy to restrain herself!

This is only one example of many instances where Heather has helped horse-rider combinations on the ground, on the flat and over jumps. It will soon reach the point (and this book will help to spread the message) where you can distinguish her students, both human and equine, from others, and I very much hope that they will all continue to promote Enlightened Equitation.

SUSAN McBANE

Like many of Heather's pupils, I was feeling pretty fed up and useless when I went on one of her courses. I knew what I wanted to achieve but couldn't get there – and although I had competed and brought on young horses successfully, there was always a missing link.

Heather provided that missing link with her revolutionary approach, her enthusiasm, encouragement, patience and humour. She has given me and hundreds of others the chance to break through that wall of frustration and to discover that perhaps we are not as useless as we thought we were.

She has the unique ability to combine Classical principles with logical, simple explanations. There are no harsh methods and no force, which is why the horses she works with become light, forward and responsive. Whatever sort of horse and pony you ride, you can achieve the same – I have seen Heather and her pupils, most of them 'ordinary' riders, produce remarkable work with ponies, cobs, Arabs, ex-racehorses... and even the rejects of the horse world.

This book is not just about dressage, though it centres on the correct progressive training of the horse. Sadly, we tend to forget that the literal meaning of 'dressage' is training, not competing. It applies to all riders and all disciplines, whether competitive or not. It you want to show jump or event, Heather's methods will improve your horse's balance and rhythm, as she proved with one of my horses.

When I first met Heather, many people in the horse world looked on her as 'that woman with the mechanical horse'. Since then, the word has spread and Heather's lecture demonstrations attract deservedly large audiences. She has also generated thought and discussions in a traditional and often hidebound world, which can only be a good thing. Some of her ideas may not find favour with all traditional teachers: for instance, she advocates using a pelham rather than a snaffle in many cases. But those who dismiss or dislike the pelham do not understand how it works or how it should be used correctly – read this book with an open mind, see the proof in the 'before and after' photographs, and draw your own conclusions.

You will enjoy this book immensely, which is another of Heather's gifts. She helped me remember that although riding offers constant challenges, we ride for the pleasure of communicating with and establishing a relationship with our horses.

Even more important, every horse you ride will thank you for reading it.

CAROLYN HENDERSON

THE RIDER

I am a fervent believer in keeping things simple. There seems to be a school of thought among riding instructors that the more complicated you can make the process of learning to ride, the more impressed the pupil will be that the instructor has mastered it. Perhaps I am wrong, but it appears to me that riding teachers never search for the simple solution. There are now all sorts of impressive-sounding 'alternative' courses that the student rider can take: courses to boost the confidence of nervous riders, where the instructor encourages them to meditate and chant mantras before mounting; courses where the instructor uses imagery and analogies by the ream to help the rider 'see' and 'feel' what is going on underneath them; courses in sports psychology, psychocybernetics, holistic approaches ... and I have pupils coming to me who have run the gamut of them all, but still end up in my yard not having reached their goal.

Very often, that goal is not to win an Olympic gold medal, but simply to ride better for the sake of the horse, as well as for safety. These people, who come from all walks of life (and my pupils range from a refuse collector to one of the world's top astrophysicists), want clear logical teaching, not convoluted explanations – or, worse still, no explanation at all. Nor do they wish to be barked at by an instructor who feels that her authority is being undermined if the pupil has the temerity to ask a question. Very often, the students who come to me are afraid to ask questions: they have been told by previous instructors that 'This how it has always been done, so don't ask why.' To their surprise and relief, I always say to new students: 'Ask as many questions as you like, because if I can't answer them, I shouldn't be teaching.'

THE BEGINNER – STAYING ABOARD

When first learning to ride, there is usually one priority in the student's mind, and that is not to fall off. It is not just the humiliation – it can actually hurt! There are some people who have so much natural bravado and confidence that the worry of falling off is never an issue, but to many – even children, who have fewer preconceptions about what might happen – the ground is a long way down and they would prefer not to have to make contact with it, other than by way of dismounting at the end of the lesson!

Surely then, **how to stay aboard is the most important piece of knowledge the rider will ever acquire in the course of her entire riding career**. Then why is it not actually taught? In most establishments, the teaching of beginners and novices is relegated to the least well-qualified teacher in their employ, yet it is beginners and novices who are

The Equisimulator

perhaps most in need of the expertise of a highly experienced instructor. It is at this stage that the foundations of the seat, and the knowledge and understanding of the aids – the basic requirements of every discipline of equestrian sport – are laid, and yet very rarely is any importance attached to the teaching of the beginner. Nevertheless, **if the right foundations are not laid at the very beginning, just like a house, the whole edifice is liable to fall down at a later date**. Any builder will tell you that it is much more difficult to underpin crumbling foundations than it is to put them in correctly in the first place. As a remedial teacher of riding, much of my work is 'underpinning', and there is no doubt that it is much harder to correct long-established faults in the rider than it is to lay down the groundwork for a fresh, new beginner.

If you are a nervous rider, do not feel that you are cowardly. Many instructors, never themselves having been afraid to ride, lose patience with such pupils because they cannot understand their reticence. I always tell nervous pupils they are, in fact, being brave, because they are confronting their fears and making themselves do something that they are apprehensive about. That takes courage.

ABSORBING THE MOVEMENT – THE EQUISIMILATOR

Nothing increases the novice or nervous pupil's confidence quicker than being shown, simply and precisely, how to stay on, how to interact with the horse's movement, so that both move as one.

For many years I had been aware that the methods of teaching that I had developed could be revolutionized by the use of a machine which would simulate the movement of the horse in walk, trot and canter. I had tried for perhaps 20 years to persuade various firms and the engineering departments of universities to build me one, but to no avail. Then, two years ago Jonathan Heyes, a pupil of mine who is an engineer, designed and built me the machines, which we named the 'Equisimulators', and everything that I hoped I could achieve with them in my teaching has been realized, and even surpassed, in reality. I do not know how I ever managed without them.

Years ago, the British Army used a movement simulator of sorts for teaching riding, but abandoned the machines because they found them to be no more use than a real horse. This would be the case now, if instructors were to place pupils on the Equisimulator and let them bounce away to their heart's content, in the hope that 'practice makes perfect'. It is the method of teaching which I use in conjunction with the machines that makes them so successful, because it breaks down the necessary action of the lower back and pelvis to absorb the movement into its separate stages. This is practised first at the halt and then in walk, gradually increasing the pace of the machine through a slow jog trot, until the rider is capable of coping with a full sitting trot equivalent to the size and stride of horse that they would normally ride. We have a separate machine which canters, as it is very difficult to make one machine for all three paces. The canter is a very different movement from walk or trot, one which is often ridden very badly for reasons we shall see in a later chapter. Teaching canter using the simulator is so much easier.

Event trainer John Thelwall, who kindly offered to act as a guinea-pig at one of my lecture demos

The Equisimulators are wonderful, too, for remedial work on riders with established faults. I run remedial workshops for such riders, **many of whom have been riding for 20 years or more and still cannot comfortably absorb the horse's movement**. Ten minutes on the simulators, being shown the precise movements of the lower back and pelvis, is often all that is necessary to correct the problems of many years. Put the rider back on a real horse, and the look of joy on their faces as they blend with the horse as one, for the first time ever, always brings immense satisfaction to me, as a teacher.

RIDING *CAN* BE TAUGHT

A couple of years ago I read an article in an American magazine. It stated that 'Riding is so personal, so subjective, that at best it can only be learnt by trial and error, with the instructor merely commenting on the learning process'. This is tantamount to saying that riding cannot actually be taught – what rubbish! A little logic and imagination was all that it took for me to work it all out. For many years, I was considered *persona non grata* in the riding teaching profession. I was outspoken, and refused on principle to take the teaching examinations, because I did not believe in what I was being made to teach. **I knew that I had found a different method, one that really did teach – not drill, army-fashion – and above all** *worked*, often drastically cutting down the initial learning period of beginner pupils because they were being taught precisely how and why. At long last, some 25 years later, my methods are being widely accepted by all who have seen me at work.

THE HORSE

I will probably be accused of being dogmatic, but after many years of experimentation I firmly believe that while there are several systems of training the horse which, correctly carried out, are perfectly humane, **there is only one way in which the rider can interact with the horse without impeding his natural movement or causing him pain**. This is the method set out in the pages of this book.

I always ask students to try putting themselves in the horse's place. Imagine that, as a young animal, you have been allowed to live a comparatively carefree existence. Suddenly, you are lunged, saddled, bridled and then mounted. Your natural reaction in the wild would be to rid yourself of anything that tried to get on your back, because it would be a predator, intent on making you its next meal. During your 'breaking in', your human handler would be trying to stifle that instinctive fear of having anything on your back. Depending on your handler's skill, this will be achieved with or without some degree of trauma, and you will then be expected to accept the unaccustomed weight of a rider without further ado.

If you are fortunate, and have a rider who is sympathetic and quiet on your back, your schooling should progress relatively unhindered.

'TRAINING' BY FORCE

But what if your rider is rough and uneducated, and gives you commands that confuse you? What if she sits like a sack of potatoes, bouncing or driving heavily with her seat on your tender and, as yet, undeveloped back muscles, so that you are sore and bruised? What if she hauls at your sensitive mouth, skinning the bars and deadening the nerve endings and kicks you in the ribs to make you go forward, when you don't even know what 'forward' means? Imagine having a pair of draw reins reeling your head in, your chin nearly touching your chest, even causing your neck muscles to break down under the strain. What would *you* do, if you were a horse? I am sure that if I were in the horse's position I would object strongly to any of these violations, and I suspect that my eventual fate would be to end up in the knackers' yard – just as it is for so many of **these unfortunate, misunderstood creatures, whose only crime is to have tried to communicate their pain, in the only way they know how.**

The rider who is moving against the horse not only makes it harder work for herself, but also causes the horse discomfort in the process. Couple this with a badly fitting saddle, and you have a recipe for considerable pain. And this pain does not last for just a few minutes: it happens any and every time the horse is ridden, for the hour, two hours or whatever that the rider is aboard, and the horse is supposed to endure it, with submission and without complaint.

There are few animals that are used as beasts of burden, the horse being the only one in most developed countries, where these days they are mostly used for recreational pleasure. We who live in such countries are supposed to be civilized and humane, and yet I am often amazed, indeed appalled, at the sheer lack of feeling and understanding shown by many riders, who are so quick to blame their horses and yet never stop to think about what they themselves might be doing to cause the 'misbehaviour'. Thankfully, there are many riders who do think, but they are often at a loss to know whom to go to for instruction. So many teachers use force to 'train' horses, and their pupils, thinking that these are the 'experts' – and such people often boast quite impressive qualifications – believe they must know what they are doing.

A KINDER WAY TO RIDE

I often receive telephone calls from 'thinking' riders, expressing their misgivings about this or that method that their trainers are advocating. **If, instinctively, something seems forced or cruel, then it *is*.** If any instructor is making you do things to your horse which you feel intuitively are wrong, then vote with your feet, and find someone who shares your view that the horse has feelings and treats him accordingly.

Anyone who thinks that they can control a horse or train him by brute force, is eventually in for a shock. A few weeks ago, I was lecturing at an event where the talk in the arena before me was given by a lady who breeds miniature ponies. Watching a fairly large man being towed off after leading these tiny equines over a small jump, was really rather comical but it drove home just how ridiculous it is for a rider to think that she can bully a horse of 17 hands or more into submission. My yard manager has enough trouble leading my pet goat, and is frequently to be seen 'water-skiing' past my indoor school as Parsley heads for her paddock in the morning!

From the safety aspect, and certainly for

Draw reins – even more severe when used, as here, with a double bridle

enjoyment, it is therefore not only in the horse's best interests but also in our own that we to learn to work with rather than against the equine species. **There is something very special about building up a relationship with a horse, to the point where you are so in tune with each other that the aids become mere thought communications.** Most riders think that such an ideal is completely beyond them: I do not believe that this is the case. Much of it boils down to education, so that the rider has a very clear understanding of the aids and of the simple biomechanics of the rider/horse interaction. Much of it can also be attributed to rider attitude.

I recently walked out of the yard of a top dressage rider and trainer, having witnessed him brutalizing his Grand Prix horse. Trying to obtain more expression in the piaffe, the rider, feeling that the horse was not 'giving' enough, thrashed him with the whip, at the same time booting him with spurs at full force and riding him straight into the walls of the indoor school. A four-year-old was being ridden in the school at the same time by another competition rider. Winched in as he was with draw reins, when the youngster started to object to his aching neck muscles, instead of giving him a break his rider beat him. This appeared to be an everyday occurrence, because nobody else in the school seemed to think that there was anything in the least bit wrong with treating horses in this way.

A friend has just bought, for a song, a truly magnificent Warmblood mare from a top dressage yard. She must have cost thousands, but was on the scrap heap at just six years old, because every time she is taken near a school, indoors or out, she shakes from head to foot. If pressed to enter the school, the mare rears to the point where she goes over backwards. My friend hopes to rehabilitate this lovely horse using the 'Enlightened' approach, so that she will eventually learn to enjoy schooling, without fear or pain.

The Classical position of balance has changed little over hundreds of years. It is the accepted way of sitting on a horse, disturbing his balance as little as possible. Nevertheless, I have several times heard trainers tell pupils: 'Don't worry too much about position, that can come later when the horse is going better.' Nothing could be further from the truth! **We are, after all, an unnatural encumbrance on the horse's back, and it behoves us as riders to make that burden as easy for the horse to carry as we are able**.

THE SADDLE

It has to be said that many saddles currently on the market do not permit the correct balance to be achieved easily. On most general purpose (GP) saddles, and more than a few dressage saddles, the stirrup bar is too far towards the front, causing the rider's thigh to be pulled forward as soon as the foot is placed in the stirrup.

I used to wonder why, when I caught sight of my reflection in the village shop window as I rode by, I still did not appear to be in the favoured ear/shoulder/hip/heel line of the Classical seat. Although my toe was placed under my knee, my heel was still several inches in front of my hip, and it was not until one day when I was riding without stirrups past the mirror in the indoor school that I noticed that the stirrup leather was actually hanging in front of my thigh. When I replaced my feet in the stirrups, and brought my legs back into the correct line, I realized that the leathers were sloping backwards from the bars, encouraging my legs to swing forward. I surmised that if the leathers were able instead to hang perpendicularly, this would allow my thigh to drop naturally, rather than it waging a constant battle with the stirrup leathers.

Classical position of balance: ear/shoulder/hip/heel in line. Thigh dropped from hip, weight softly, not forced, into heel

General purpose saddle

Saddles have a lot to answer for. While most are well made by fine craftsmen, not all are designed to assist the rider, who ends up fighting the very tool which is supposed to be there to help. I have taught many riders who believed themselves to be hopeless, but were amazed by the immediate difference in their position when given the opportunity of riding on a saddle purposely designed to aid posture and balance.

Another anomaly in saddle design occurs with the seat. It has always seemed illogical to me to make the saddle seat out of a foam which is resilient and springy, top it with a drum-tight piece of leather, and then expect the rider to sit to a big-moving horse! The movement simply reverberates up through the whole saddle, making it very difficult for the rider to absorb.

Rider's thigh pulled forwards by placement of stirrup bar

Showing angle of stirrup leather necessary for rider to sit in ear/shoulder/hip/heel balance

My dressage saddle design. Note stirrup leather hangs perpendicularly without effort on part of rider

HELP YOURSELF!

I eventually designed my own saddle for use in my school, and I have been very pleased with the assistance that it affords the rider. It is based on the old Portuguese Classical saddles but with modern adaptations, giving unrivalled comfort and balance – indeed, it is difficult to sit badly in it. It has been criticized by one or two purists, who believe that the saddle should offer the rider little or no support and that to do so is cheating both yourself as a rider and your teacher. I disagree. Few people in this day and age have the time to spend the hours on a horse which are required to develop the poise and musculature that permit the rider to sit with ease on almost any saddle. Most horse owners spend, at best, an hour in the saddle daily, and riding school clients

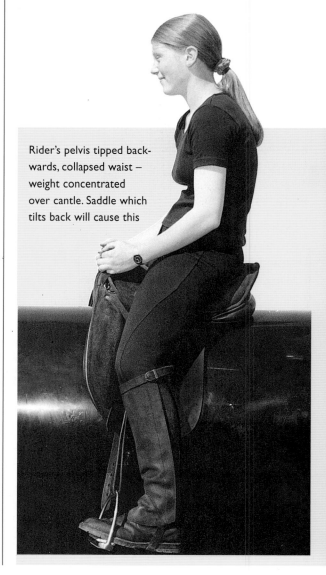

Rider's pelvis tipped backwards, collapsed waist – weight concentrated over cantle. Saddle which tilts back will cause this

far less; **I therefore believe that it is better to have saddles which assist the rider to achieve an easy balance – mainly for the sake of the horse, who cannot perform correctly if the rider is wriggling around on his back, fighting to maintain position**.

Apart from leg position, the saddle should also aid a central balance. If the rider is tipped backwards, her weight will concentrate over the cantle, depressing the horse's sensitive loins. If the rider is tipped too far forwards, this will not only render her seat weak but will also load the horse's forehand which, through schooling, we are

Stirrups that I prefer to use in my school – larger tread area helps students to maintain lower leg position – foot has less tendency to slip through

trying to lighten. The rider must sit midway between the two points, and in such a way that a line could be drawn through her ear, shoulder, hip and heel. Then, if the horse were whisked away from under her, she would land on her feet in a standing position, but with her knees slightly bent.

Many riders find this position quite difficult to achieve, and there are various schools of thought currently being debated that question the need for the rider to have the thigh in a relatively vertical position, as it is deemed

Rider tipping too far forwards. Saddle which is too high at the back will tip rider forward

Rider leaning back, lower leg slipping forward. Also caused by backward tilting saddle, again concentrating weight over cantle

unnatural. I would point out that **the very act of sitting on a horse is unnatural for a human being**, as we rarely open our hips sideways except when riding. To have too great an angle in the knee would prevent us from achieving easily the immensely subtle use of the seat as an aid, which is explained in Chapter 6. To achieve a deep knee position requires sideways openness in the hip joint, and also in the inside of the thigh where it joins the body, where many riders are rather tight (see page 24 for how to stretch these areas). This will cause problems relating to the uprightness of the torso and position of the lower leg.

THE SEAT

There has been much discussion, indeed argument, over the 'bits' of our anatomy on which we sit. Students end up in a state of confusion, because one instructor tells them one thing and another something completely different, to the point where they do not know who to believe. **Confused pupils cause confused horses; confused horses turn into resistant, truculent ones, who then get the blame for the rider's ineptitude**.

Considerable debate has raged over the years about the concept of the 'three point seat'. There are two schools of thought on the subject.

1   The first argues that the three points constitute the two seatbones and the pubic arch. This means that the pubic arch, the bony third point of the tripod, is in constant contact with the front arch of the saddle. Most riders find this uncomfortable, to say the least, and in order to achieve such a position, the lower back is hollowed excessively, forming a forced lordosis (forward curvature of the spine) rather than the natural, slight curve of the small of the back. As a result, the flexion afforded by this area – which is of paramount importance, as it is the means by which we are able to adhere without effort to the saddle – is negated.

2   The second school of thought states that the three-point seat constitutes the whole area between the seatbones and the pubic arch, but does not insist on the pubic arch being in constant contact with the saddle. I can accept this, as it still permits free rotation of the pelvis in order to absorb the horse's movement.

I prefer to think of the position at the halt as resting on *six* points; the two seatbones, the insides of the thighs, and the calves, which are in light contact with the horse's sides. In this way, the weight is spread around as large a surface area as possible, the rider being largely responsible for her own weight, with no large concentration directly on the horse's back.

THE RIDER'S POSITION

Even the most experienced and skilled riders need to constantly monitor their positions. Make a top-to-toe check list with mirrors, or get a friend to video you.

THE HEAD

Being a heavy part of the body, the head can make a significant difference to the position and balance of the rider by being carried correctly. I have found that there are several factors that can affect the carriage of the head, the first and most common being the length and set of the rider's neck.

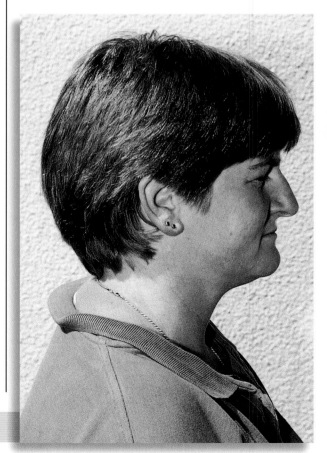

Short, straight neck

- If the neck is short, and growing straight up from the shoulders, there is rarely any problem.
- When the neck is longer and set more to the front of the shoulders, the rider often has a tendency to jut the chin forwards. Because the head is in front of the line of balance, the whole of the torso can be toppled out of alignment.

I have discovered that jutting the chin forward can also be a habit developed by the wearing of plastic chin cups of the kind to be found on jockey skull caps. Many riders find them irritating, and unconsciously poke their chin into the cup to keep the latter in place. In most cases, the rider's head returns to a normal position almost as soon as the offending object is removed from the chinstrap.

Tilting the head sideways is another common deviation from the normal head carriage. In some cases, I have found that it contributes significantly to the rider collapsing the hip on that side. By bringing the head back to an upright position, the body tends to stretch up with it on that side, thereby eliminating two faults with one simple correction.

A pupil of mine, from the European Space Agency Riding Club in Holland, had a habit of staring at the indoor school ceiling. I initially put this human version of 'stargazing' down to his occupation! The student was the proud possessor of a bushy ginger beard, which appeared to make the chin cup of his hat slip. By raising his head and looking at the roof, he had prevented this from happening. Removing the chin cup had the desired effect, and his head position returned to normal.

Another common phenomenon, found particularly among dressage riders, is that of **the nodding head. This is most unsightly and totally unnecessary, but seems to have become almost a fashion in the dressage arena**; certainly judges do not seem to pass comment on it, or object to it in any way. The problem stems not from the carriage of the head, but from the action of the seat, due to a backward-tilted and driving pelvis (this is discussed in detail in Chapter 3).

When the head is carried too still and erect, as if balancing a book on the head in a deportment class, it produces a rather forced, stiff-necked appearance.

I have always had problems with the carriage of my own head, having a long and slightly forward-set neck. I was often told by instructors 'Neck into the back of the collar', but that seemed to stiffen it even more. I also have a habit of tilting my head slightly to the right, which, as a remedial teacher of riding trying to correct such faults, I found absolutely maddening!

I finally found a solution, thanks to a friend who is an Alexander Technique teacher as well as a riding instructor. I had always felt that I was blocking the horse's movement slightly, even though absorbing it through my lower back had never been a problem. When I sat on a horse after being shown how to release my head and neck, I could literally feel an extra lift in the horse's stride, as if I had previously been squashing the movement slightly. Amazingly, I could even feel an extra spring and lightness in my own step on the ground! All it required to release my

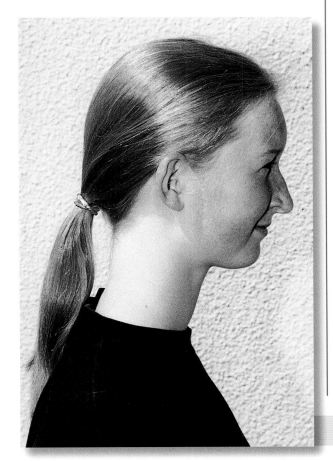

Long forward-set neck

head was to allow it to oscillate barely perceptibly on its axis at the top of my neck. This does not produce the 'nodding head syndrome' as it is so slight, but although I still have to be aware of it and remember to allow my head to 'float', I now look and feel much more natural from the shoulders up when I ride.

THE SHOULDERS

The most frequent problem encountered in the shoulders is that of rounding and hunching. Riders who spend long hours working at a desk or computer are particularly prone to hunching their shoulders, and this does tend to manifest itself when they are mounted on a horse. Rounded shoulders also occur as a side effect of having the reins too short. Pupils are constantly exhorted by some instructors to shorten their reins, with the result that their arms straighten, their upper body rounds forwards, and their shoulders become aching and tired, because they are being forced to carry the weight of the arms unnaturally.

It is often said that **when riding we should mirror as closely as possible what we would do on the ground**. I have often amused pupils with a

Rider's arms too straight, forcing back to round and shoulders to unnaturally carry the full weight of the arms

'Pram pushing hands'

simple demonstration to illustrate this. I mimic the posture of the pupil with hunched back and arms out in front of her body, suggesting that if one were to walk along the high street of any town in such a position, it would attract a few curious glances! Instead, if one were to walk with the upper arms hanging perpendicularly and hands carried just in front of the stomach, it would not warrant a single glance. By merely asking the rider to bring the arm back to the point where the upper arm is perpendicular, it is possible to correct the whole upper body position in just one move.

THE ARMS AND HANDS

The arms, then, need to be carried in as natural a position as possible, with the elbow, wrist and finger joints supple in order to maintain a light and elastic contact with the horse's mouth. It therefore drives me to distraction when I see instructors teaching pupils to shorten the reins as described above, to the point where their hands are halfway up the horse's neck, with their arms locked straight and shoulders rounded, thereby destroying the elastic connection to the mouth. Turning the hands inwards, as if pushing a

pram, causes the elbows to be turned outwards. This not only looks ugly, but also leads to unsteady hands that chop up and down at every stride, disturbing the contact and provoking justified resistance in the horse. The hands should be held with the thumbs uppermost and the wrists very slightly rounded inwards.

The position of the hands causes some confusion; often pupils are made to ride with their hands too high, and in some cases too far apart, as if pushing a wheelbarrow. The FEI dressage rules state that 'The hands should be held low and close together, without, however, touching either each other or the horse.' I feel that even this is too restrictive. The need for a straight line from bit to elbow is an accepted criterion when riding. With this in mind, I like to teach that there are three hand positions, to suit the horse's head position.

1 When the horse is being worked long and low, as with a young horse, or during warming up or cooling down, the hands should be low on either side of the neck.
2 In a novice horizontal balance, the hands should be carried just above and in front of the pommel of the saddle.

Stiff wrists, hands turning outwards, broken line of contact from elbow to bit

Correct position of hands, thumbs uppermost, wrists slightly rounded

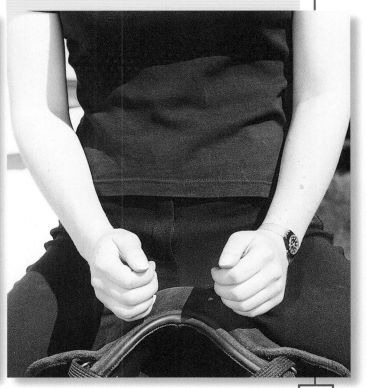

3 For the higher head carriage of the advanced horse, the hands should be carried a couple of inches higher, level with or just below the rider's waist.

The latter is preferred by some schools, but the most desirable of all is when the high school horse is in such a state of self-carriage that the rider can practise the ***descente des mains* of the Classical masters**, when the hands will be lowered again to the level of the novice outline, **with the reins in loops, the horse so light in hand that the weight of the reins and the merest vibration of them is sufficient to control him in the highest state of collection**.

Rider's lower leg 'clinging like a wet cloth', quietly wrapped around the horse's sides

THE LEGS

The legs are the main propulsive aid to enable us to ask the horse to move forward, but they also ask for sideways movement and control the swing of the quarters. Again, some controversy surrounds the use of the legs, mostly arising out of misinterpretation.

Weakness in the lower leg is a prime cause of instability in the rider's overall position, and usually stems from a lack of muscle tone, as well as from tightness in the hip joints. We rarely need to open our hip joints sideways except when riding, and so many riders find it difficult to encompass the shape of the horse, with the result that the thighs and knees are pinched inwards, forcing the lower leg away from the horse's sides.

Some instructors actually advise pupils to place a hand under the thigh, and pull the muscle out from underneath, so that the thigh lies flatter on the saddle. This is all very well in theory, but doing so also tightens the hips, turns the knee in and forces the lower leg out, so that the sole of the boot becomes clearly visible – the very opposite of what we need to achieve in order to open the hip joints and allow

Pulling thigh muscle out behind turns knee in and forces lower leg away from horse's sides

'Some instructors actually advise pupils to place a hand under the thigh, and pull the muscle out from underneath…'

25

I use few analogies, generally preferring a specific explanation, but one that I do like to borrow is given by Sally Swift in her book Centred Riding. *This is the idea of imagining that you have a bungee rope attached to your hat, which suggests the notion that you are suspended lightly on the horse, with your legs draped around his sides, and your body poised and toned but without rigidity anywhere, able to absorb fluidly the movement under you at all paces, and with ease.*

the lower leg to 'cling like a wet cloth, but without gripping', as many German schools advise.

Purely as a remedial measure, in order to enable the hip joints to open, I ask pupils to open the knee slightly and, if necessary, roll the little toe outwards so that it is slightly lower than the big toe. This will bring the calf into quiet contact with the lower half of the horse's ribcage. As the hip joints become more supple and open, the knee will return to facing forwards and the foot will be able to return to a level position. As far as the rider's conformation will allow, the foot should always point forwards, not outwards, as this would bring the back of the calf rather than the inside into contact and encourage the lower leg to 'grip up' in use.

BALANCE

One of the commonest causes of lack of balance is that the rider tips forward. This may be due to one of several factors:

- If nervousness is the cause, and frequently it is, **the rider assumes a 'foetal crouch' – or 'fatal crouch', as I prefer to call it**!
- Collapsing the ribcage and rounding out the lower back is another fault, which is not only unsightly but also makes the rider a heavy burden to carry, as she will be like the proverbial floppy 'sack of potatoes' in the saddle.

This problem is often associated with slack stomach muscles, so I have a simple but effective remedy for riders in this category: I take one of those back supports that incorporate a firm pad, and place it on the front, not the back! This supports the stomach and prevents any collapsing of the ribcage. It is purely a remedial tool to assist the rider initially in adopting a more upright posture, and I find that it works well.

- Riders who shorten the reins to the extent that their hands are placed well up the horse's neck will also find that the upper body is pulled forwards. Often, when I first ask riders who have become established in this position to sit upright, they feel as if they are leaning halfway back to the horse's tail, when in fact they have only moved the torso by a couple of inches.

  Invariably, as the body becomes upright, the lower leg swings forwards, and the knee wants to rise, because of tightness in the torso/thigh joint. Work without stirrups, preferably on the lunge, is the easiest way to stretch this area. Allowing the legs to hang, actually pointing the toes downwards, and holding for about 30 seconds at a time will help stretch the torso/thigh joint without undue strain. Take care, however, that the upper body does not topple forward again as the legs drop down.

ASYMMETRY

Crookedness in the rider produces crookedness in the horse. I was astonished several years ago to hear an international judge at a seminar commenting only on the horse's crookedness, without mentioning the underlying cause – **the famous rider on board was sitting so far out to the right that it was *impossible* for the horse to move straight**. Unequal weight distribution on the seatbones makes the horse want to veer to the side on which the weight is concentrated.

Asymmetry in the rider can take one of several forms. For example:

- If the rider collapses the right hip she will weight the seatbone on that side more than the other.
- Alternatively, collapsing the right hip makes the seat slide outwards to the left, so that the weight is transferred to that seatbone.
- Occasionally, the whole upper body will twist to the inside, even when riding on a straight line. Again, this will weight the outside seatbone and cause the horse to drift through his outside shoulder.

Correction of asymmetry requires constant vigilance from the instructor, who ideally should stand in a corner of the school where it is possible to monitor the rider easily from in front and behind. The rider must learn to recognize the feel of sitting with the weight distributed equally on both seatbones, and do a frequent mental check to ask, 'Am I sitting square?' For riders with an established collapsing hip problem, I again employ my back support belt, which this time I place on the rider's side. The firm pad in the belt makes it difficult, and certainly uncomfortable, to collapse the hip, so it is helpful in re-establishing the correct posture. Only by making the rider aware of what she is doing, and readjusting the position frequently, will the problem be resolved.

Rider collapsing hip

INTERACTION WITH THE HORSE'S MOVEMENT

The most important part of learning to ride – as I'm sure any novice rider would agree – is learning to stay on board, yet the actual method of doing so is never really explained. 'Sit deeper', 'Go with the movement', and 'Relax your back' are all instructions that pupils receive, yet to a novice such statements are about as meaningful as if they were spoken in a foreign language. 'Sit deeper' usually means that the student stiffens and tries to sit more heavily in the saddle, bouncing as a result. 'Go with the movement' and the pupil tries too hard, moving about more than is necessary. 'Relax your back' implies that the rider should collapse the ribcage and become floppy.

ABSORBING THE MOVEMENT – EARLY EXPERIMENTS

As a young teenager, I worked out for myself the precise movement of the rider's lower back and pelvis by watching Western films. I had noticed that the cowboys seemed to sit very much at ease in the saddle, and were tall and straight. I had also seen the great Portuguese maestro Nuño Oliveira at the 1966 Horse of the Year Show, and had been stunned by his effortless artistry. I knew that this was how I too wished to ride, and as at that time no one seemed able or willing to help me achieve my aim, I realized that I would have to find out as much as possible for myself.

Watching the better riders in Western films, it soon became apparent to me that to achieve adhesion to the saddle they were doing something with the lower back that I had certainly not been taught. I set about experimenting, and one day it happened – I achieved the easy adherence to the saddle that I had been seeking. It took place as I was playing about on a friend's race exercise saddle, with

my stirrups up at racing length. I tried to sit to the trot for a few strides, flexing my lower back as I did so, and eureka! I remained glued to the saddle. With virtually no leg to hang on with due to the shortness of the stirrup leathers, I would have fallen off, but this flexion allowed me to remain in place

Nuño Oliveira

without difficulty. I remember dashing back to the stables to replace the saddle with my usual one, and then practising the movement over and again for the next few minutes, until I was sure that it happened every time.

Over the next few days I experimented similarly with the canter, and realized very quickly that by 'rowing with the shoulders', as I had previously been doing to prevent my seat leaving the saddle, I had actually been impeding my horse (we will be looking at the reasons for this later in this chapter).

Friends at the time noticed a drastic improvement in my riding, and asked whether I could teach them to do the same. It seemed only logical to analyse what I was doing myself, in order to be able to explain it simply to my friends. I soon realized that **it was the synchronization of the movements of my lower back and pelvis with the movement of the horse's back that enabled me to remain quietly glued to the saddle – appearing, in fact, to be doing almost nothing at all**.

I have always since taught in this way, but my teaching was further enhanced when I became interested in Classical equitation and sought the help of Captain Desi Lorent, himself a student of Nuño Oliveira. Desi taught me to be aware not only of the up-and-down movement of the horse, but also of the side-to-side dip of his back. I had, it seemed, been both correctly synchronizing the oscillation of my lower back and allowing my pelvis to move with the horse, but had been largely unaware of the latter, the significance of which we will be examining in Chapter 4.

> *I recently received a video from a rider who is having many problems with her young mare, which she has backed herself and has attempted to school. The owner obviously cares, but through ignorance of the facts believes that the horse, which has been deemed stubborn and lazy, is to blame. The truth is that the owner's riding is so crude that it is totally blocking the horse, who is not being unwilling but is patently trying to communicate that she cannot go forwards with such treatment. From the video, it is apparent that the horse hasn't a clue what the rider is asking, never having been taught to respond to clear and consistent aids – truly a case of the blind leading the blind, and sadly all too common.*

While I fully accept that are several successful ways in which to train the horse, as I have already stated, over the last few years I have become increasingly convinced that there is only one way to ride which interacts biomechanically with the horse's back in a way which does not impede him. If only more riders would take note of this fact, they would encounter far fewer of the resistances and evasions that unsympathetic riding will provoke. One of my pupils remarked that riding a horse and interacting wrongly with its movement is a bit like trying to canoe upriver against the current, but there is one big difference – the river doesn't feel pain, and therefore doesn't object!

CARRYING THE RIDER

When schooling the horse for dressage – or any other discipline for that matter, even if only to render him more obedient and pleasant to ride out hacking – we are seeking to encourage him to carry us and move forward with ease. An uneducated horse carrying a rider pulls himself along by his front legs, instead of propelling himself forward with his hind end. To use motoring parlance, we must therefore convert the horse from a front-engined model to a rear-engined version. The unschooled horse will carry the rider with his back hollowed and head raised, his hindlegs trailing out behind 'in the next county'. This is the very opposite of what is required to enable the horse to carry the rider and propel himself forward with the minimum of effort.

Try a little experiment. Get down on all fours and raise your head a little, which will hollow your back; now attempt to walk forwards, which you will find quite difficult. Next, lower your head, when your back will raise and round. It will now be easy to walk forwards, because your 'hindlegs' will be able to step under your body, instead of trailing out behind.

This, in practice, is what we must teach the horse to do. He must lower his head and step under his body mass with this hindlegs. In doing so, he raises his back, creating a bridge on which the rider sits, deeply but lightly.

RESISTANCE AND THE DRIVING SEAT
If the horse's back is depressed through a heavy, driving seat, the head will raise and the hindlegs disengage – and yet teaching of the driving seat

Raising head, hollowing back and attempting to walk forwards with difficulty!

is still very common. It does not makes sense to 'scoop' back and forth with the seat bones, as if scooping icecream out of a tub, when we want the horse to round his back, not hollow it. The whole concept is illogical. One prominent teaching body actually advocates that the rider press down with the seat as the horse's back rises, in the belief that the horse will react by raising his back in resistance to the pressure of the seat. It is perfectly true that the horse will resist into pressure: anyone who has had a horse stand on her foot and tried to push him off will testify to this! However, the area of the horse's back under the saddle contains a reflex point which, when pressure is applied, causes the back to drop in response, in turn raising the head. The rider then resorts to 'sawing' on the reins in order to lower the horse's head again, thereby pulling in the horse at the front and restricting his free, forward movement.

If a doctor tests our reflexes by tapping the one situated just below the knee, provided we know each time that the tap is going to happen, after a few blows we can deactivate the reflex by resistance, tensing up the muscles and holding the calf back tightly against the shin of the other leg. The horse can do the same with his back reflexes, so after a short time he will begin to raise his back in defence, but will not yield in his jaw. The rider still has to pull in the front end, which is why the remark 'Short in the neck' is so common in dressage test judging.

Raising the back in this way will develop what I term 'resistance muscle', which is solid and unyielding, more like the muscle of a body builder, when what is needed is 'gymnastic muscle', which is flexible and enables fluidity and expression in the movement. This can only happen when the horse is relaxed in his lower jaw, the rider maintaining a light, 'feeling' contact and mirroring the movements of the horse's back as closely as possible with her own.

Since dressage has emerged as a fast-growing sport in countries that have no tradition of Classical riding, misinterpretation of Continental methods has caused a lot of harsh riding to appear. The driving seat is perhaps the worst, because it has several further effects on the horse's way of going:

■ The effect on many more placid horses, quite apart from the ugly style of riding that it produces, will be that they slow down, or even stop, so that the horse is thought of as lazy,

Lowering head, raising back, Tim can now step under and walk forwards easily

requiring a lot of leg, whip and spur to galvanize him into action.

■ On the other hand, sensitive blood horses such as Thoroughbreds and Arabians will often react to this way of riding by fizzing up, dropping the back and scooting out from under the rider's seatbones, quickly developing a reputation for being 'hot'. Speed rather than impulsion is therefore generated, although currently there seems to be some confusion in the dressage world, as to the difference between the two.

RESISTANCE AND SITTING STILL

It is logical to suppose that **by mirroring the horse's back movements as closely as possible with our own, we will move together as one unit**. This does not, however, mean sitting still. Many instructors try to teach their pupils to sit still, but this causes the rider to bounce stiffly in the saddle, as she will not be able to absorb the upward thrust of the horse's stride in any pace other than walk. When the rider bounces, the horse 'boards' up

his muscles in defence against the discomfort. A rigid back makes for an uncomfortable ride and the horse will never be able to move with real suppleness and swing, which is a prerequisite for any progress to be made in training.

ABSORBING THE MOVEMENT – PUTTING IT INTO PRACTICE

So how do we absorb the movement in a way that will not hinder the horse? I teach this on my Equisimulators, which are machines that replicate the movement of the horse in all three paces (see page 13). I find them invaluable, because I can initially manipulate the rider's body, by showing her the range of flexion in the lower back. Starting at the halt, I can teach a total beginner to adhere to the saddle in sitting trot, and to rise to the trot in balance, often in less than an hour. Think how much discomfort this saves the real horse!

I always demonstrate the range of flexion in the lower back by getting on the machine myself first. Many students look at me in disbelief! 'My back won't do that,' is often the protest, 'it is far too stiff!' I generally reply that the stiffness is in the rider's head, which is usually the case. Few riders cannot

3

manage the movement when they are shown precisely how to do it. Often, riders who are stiff in the back in everyday life find that flexing the back correctly when on the horse strengthens their back muscles and alleviates pain.

I then demonstrate how the horse's back moves – not in one solid piece, but in two halves; the Equisimulator has been designed to imitate this, as well. **Fortunately, the Almighty had the foresight to design the human rear end similarly, in two halves, making it relatively easy for us to allow our seatbones to synchronize with the rise and fall of the horse's back.**

THE WALK

The walk is a four-time gait, the left hind moving first, followed by the left fore, then the right hind and the right fore, producing a smooth forward movement with no upward thrust which requires no effort on the part of the rider in order for her to sit to it. Having said that, it is all too easy to block the horse's back muscles and impede his forwardness by pushing against the movement with the seat, or even by sitting too passively. The horse then saunters along at his own pace, without any real control from the rider. It is therefore essential that we synchronize our own movements with those of the horse, so that when we do deliberately interrupt the flow – by use of the seat not as a *driving* aid, but as a *retarding* aid – the horse feels the difference and reacts accordingly (this use of the seat is explained in Chapter 5).

This synchronization in walk is achieved merely by allowing the horse to move your seatbones. As his back dips on the left side, the left seatbone is lowered, and as his left hind strikes the ground and pushes upwards, the left seatbone will be pushed up and forwards. Likewise, the right seatbone will be lowered as the right side of the back dips, and pushed up and forwards as the right side rises. Therefore, as

the horse walks one seatbone will be lowered and the other raised, simultaneously, not by any action of the rider but solely by the movement of the horse. **Any movement of the rider additional to that offered by the horse is superfluous, and will also interrupt the horse's rhythm.** It is the action of the rider's *legs*, not the seat, which maintains or increases impulsion.

SITTING TROT

The trot is a pace of two-time, so that the horse's legs move in diagonal pairs, with a moment of suspension in between the spring from one pair to the other. If the rider does not make a compensatory movement with her lower back and pelvis, she will bounce in the saddle, and then grip to stay on. Unlike the walk, which has no upward thrust, in trot the rider will be lifted out of the saddle at each stride and will return to it, courtesy of gravity, with a bump. The precise synchronization of the back that I learned as a youngster from watching Western films never seems to be taught, and as a result some pretty peculiar compromises arise, as the student struggles to find a way to help her adhere to the saddle.

The driving seat again

The driving seat (see page 29) is perhaps the most common method employed to absorb the movement in sitting trot and canter, partly because it is encouraged by instructors. 'Tuck your tail under' and 'Polish the saddle' are popular commands and this is just what happens. The rider tilts the pelvis backwards, rendering the lower back incapable of flexion, and slides her seatbones back and forth along the saddle, often causing considerable discomfort until the skin of the buttocks becomes hardened to the friction. As the seatbones slide forward together, the knees drop down, and as they slide back again, the knees come up. This causes the lower leg to

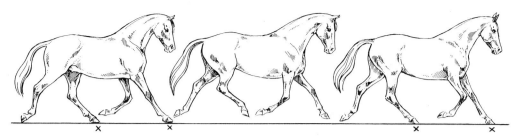

waggle at every stride, irritating the horse in the process, particularly if the rider is wearing spurs.

The driving seat is also the cause of the ugly 'nodding head syndrome' so often seen in dressage riders (see page 19). Because the lower back has been made rigid by angling the pelvis backwards, if the rider is not to bounce the movement has to come out somewhere. The next available flexible 'bits' are the neck and shoulders, which therefore have to take up the movement – hence the nodding head. Nothing looks worse when riding than excessive movement *anywhere*, but I am bemused as to why dressage riders of all people, who must have been attracted to the sport for aesthetic reasons in the first place, do not seem to realize how horrible the nodding head looks. What is more, how on earth do they see where they are going?

Because the seat is moving forwards and back as one unit, whereas the horse's back is moving as two, the rider will inadvertently impede the horse. As the horse's back raises on one side, the rider's seatbones, moving together instead of separately, will depress the back and cause it to hollow.

Absorbing the trot correctly

When the rider absorbs the movement correctly, she will be making four separate movements of the lower back and pelvis. Her back will flex in on the upward beat of the stride, and then straighten on the down beat – thereby shortening the spine (by flexing it inwards) by roughly the same amount that the horse's back is rising, and lengthening it again, by the same amount as the horse's back is falling – all in time with the one, two, one, two rhythm of the trot. This keeps the rider's seat on the same plane as the horse's back. In order to allow it to function unhindered, the seatbones also synchronize with the rise and fall of each side of the horse's back, in the same way as in walk.

The driving seat in trot and canter. Note that in both cases the horse is looking tense; the rider's seatbones have slid back, causing the knee to grip up and the lower leg to slide back

You can try this out easily by sitting on a stool. Flex your back as in the photograph (left), and then straighten it again as in the second photograph (right). Now flex your back again, but accentuate the left hip forward a little, so that you feel the left seatbone rotate on to its front edge. Return the pelvis to upright by straightening the spine again. Now flex the spine once again, this time rotating the right hip a little further forward than the left, then return again to upright. These are the four movements that comprise sitting trot: left hip rotated forward, straighten spine again, right hip rotated forward, straighten spine again. The feeling is of your seatbones being walked forwards (not sideways across the saddle) by the horse, with your back acting as a shock absorber for the upward thrust. If you place your hand in the small of your back as you try this, you will feel a small oscillation there, which acts like a spring to accept the rebound of the trot, keeping your seat softly 'glued' to the saddle.

Absorbing the trot correctly: (left) the back flexing in on the upward beat of the stride; (right) and straightening on the downward beat

In this way, the lower leg remains still, as does the upper body, giving the whole picture *the appearance of being still*. As I have tried to explain to several eminent teachers who try to teach their pupils to sit still, **there is a big difference between actually sitting completely still on a horse, when the rider will unavoidably bounce, and *appearing* to be still, which is the result of horse and rider moving together as one unit**.

Teaching sitting trot

I have often taken clinics where we have hired the facilities of riding schools, and have had the opportunity to watch the odd lesson in progress, normally where beginners or novice riders are being

taught. When sitting trot is being taught, I have at times had great difficulty restraining myself from rushing into the lesson and taking over. More often that not, the instructor will have a class of novices bouncing around in sitting trot without stirrups, circuiting the school for minutes on end, usually clutching onto the pommel of the saddle for dear life and leaning in at a precarious angle around corners, all in the mistaken belief that it will deepen the rider's seat. If this were the case, why do I regularly get riders on my remedial courses who have been riding for 20 years or more and yet still avoid sitting trot like the plague, because they have never mastered it? The same happens to a lesser degree in canter.

After I have taught a student the breakdown of sitting trot on the Equisimulator, and she has mastered it easily on the machine, I put her on a real horse. If she is a complete beginner, it will be on the lunge, but for remedial work I can do this just as easily off the lunge. Instead of performing umpteen circuits of the school in sitting trot, I ask the rider to make frequent transitions back to walk, and then up to trot again, often doing no more than half a dozen strides of trot before returning to walk, walking for a few

whole circuit of the school, and ultimately for as long as you wish. By doing it *gradually* you will not lose balance, and therefore confidence. If for any reason you find it difficult to return to walk, and start to bounce, go into rising trot, then return to walk. In Chapter 9, I will be showing you how to use your body weight to make a downward transition to walk from rising trot, so that sitting trot is avoided.

RISING TROT

Rising trot is another area of teaching where diversity, and therefore confusion, abounds. **To me, rising trot is first and foremost a way of relieving the horse's back of weight,** particularly over long distances when out hacking, when riding a young horse whose back has not yet developed sufficiently to use sitting trot, when warming up, when giving the horse a break, or when cooling down again after a schooling session.

Many riders, particularly novices, rise excessively high, locking the knee in the process so that they are literally rising 'up and down' – hence the bobbing head. Rising in this way brings the seat back into the saddle with the pelvis in an upright position, which will almost certainly ensure that the rider's weight bangs heavily down on the back of the saddle over the horse's loins, causing him discomfort.

Instead, the rider should absorb the upward thrust of the stride, allowing the hips to move forward towards the pommel and back to the saddle as if on an arc, with the pelvis returning to the saddle at a slightly forward angle and the shoulders very slightly in front of the vertical. In this way, the seat is ready to receive the movement of the horse, which will propel the hips forwards, then back, to touch down as light as a feather. The rider does not need to make

strides, and then moving back into trot again. In this way, the rider picks up the sideways swing of the horse's back, which is more pronounced during a progressive transition, and can synchronize easily with the first few strides of sitting trot, before generally, losing it, and starting to bounce and grip up.

Practising sitting trot

As before, try this for yourself. If you can keep it for the first four strides to start with, it will not be long before you can hold it for the full six or so strides, before returning to walk. Gradually, you will be able to keep it going for eight or ten strides, and then 12 or 14 strides, and so on, until you have the strength and poise to be able to sit easily to the trot for a

Students often laugh at me when I see a rider hacking down our dug-out Devon lanes and remark on the rider's ability – or, more often – inability to rise to the trot. 'But how can you tell, you can only see her head and shoulders?' is the usual question. I can tell easily: if the head is on a steady, level plane, then I know that the trot is being performed correctly. If the head is bobbing up and down like a cork on water, I know that the action of the rider is incorrect.

an effort to heave her seat out of the saddle, working against the movement, rather than with it, which in the process also hinders the horse.

Some instructors insist on the pupil maintaining an upright position of the torso and pelvis throughout all phases of the rising trot. This is a mistake, because the conformation of the rider also needs to be taken into account.

Rider is too upright in the upper body and rising too high

Rider has returned to the saddle with an upright pelvis; her weight drops onto the cantle, depressing the back

- Riders with short, straight spines will find it easier to maintain a more upright torso position, although care must still be exercised to ensure that their weight does not land heavily in the saddle.
- However, riders with long, willowy spines will find it almost impossible not to fall behind the movement if made to ride in this way, unless they swing their hips forwards and back with considerable gusto, unbalancing both themselves and the horse.

I have heard instructors teaching this excessive swing of the hips as a way of increasing impulsion. **I fail to see how thrusting your backside vigorously through thin air can create anything other than a disturbance to the horse.** It may cause some more sensitive types to scoot along faster, but speed has nothing to do with impulsion! We will be looking at this subject in Chapter 10. The one exception to the 'upper body not upright' rule is when riding a very big moving horse or a highly schooled one. There is likely to be so much upward spring in the stride that the rider's upper body will remain upright as the pelvis is propelled forward to a greater degree by the bigger movement. Be careful not to move more than the horse dictates; riding a horse with this amount of movement requires a lot of body control.

Care also needs to be taken that the pelvis does not tip backwards on returning to the saddle as, again, a lot of weight will land over the loins. Using the Equisimulators, I ask pupils to place a hand underneath their seat and then to experiment by rising the trot in all the different ways I have outlined above, so that they can feel what the horse would feel for themselves. They are always very surprised, and often quite shocked, to experience what is a distinct and dramatic change in their weight distribution. I often demonstrate the effect on the horse by rising in this way on a very forward-going horse, having first shown the correct way. The horse slows immediately, to the point where I have to use a lot of leg. How many horses, ridden in this way, are blamed for being lazy, when it is the *rider* who is preventing the horse from going actively forward?

THE CANTER

The canter is a pace of three-time. The sequence of footfalls is outside hind, inside hind and outside fore together, followed by inside fore, and then a

moment of suspension. Riders nearly always work far too hard to absorb the movement in canter, either rowing back and forth with their shoulders, or once again 'polishing the saddle'. **In canter, we are seeking to encourage the horse to make each step a little jump, rounding and lifting his back in a convex shape and lightening the forehand.** When the rider's shoulders row back and forth, or the seat polishes the saddle, the seat itself will be scooping in a concave manner, opposing the convex shape and pressing downwards heavily on to the saddle, thereby encouraging the horse to hollow rather than round.

The correct way to sit to the canter is altogether much less effort, for both rider and horse. Again, sitting on a stool, flex your spine in, and then out to straight again, on a count of three, feeling how the pelvis rotates forwards and then back to upright in the process. This flexion is all that is necessary to absorb the movement of the canter. The upper body stays upright, the lower leg wrapping quietly around the horse's sides to maintain impulsion, giving an overall impression of stillness. Logically, the pivoting seatbones are mirroring the changing angles of the horse's back as it rises and falls, so instead of driving downwards they are permitting the back to round up to the seat.

How much flexion?

The difference between riding a young, green horse (or an older uneducated one) and a supple, well-schooled horse is similar to that between driving a bumpy old tractor and a Rolls Royce.

A horse that is hollow, heavy on his feet and pulling himself along on the forehand will be less easy to sit on than one which is propelling himself forward from behind, raising and 'bridging' the back, with the joints of his limbs acting as shock absorbers as they spring elastically under him. I demonstrate this by taking a dressage whip and bending it so that it is concave, then flipping it up to convex. This is much the same as a horse's back will do to the rider, if it is hollow. If instead the horse is rounding his back already and stepping well under his body, there will be much less 'flip' of his back under the rider, which naturally requires less flexion of her lower back. Therefore, the more educated the horse, the less the rider's back has to flex to absorb the movement, because although there will be more upward spring as the horse comes into collection, the hoof has less impact with the ground.

I am often castigated by my peers for teaching this deliberate flexion of the lower back to absorb the horse's movement, but the amount varies greatly according to the stage of training. I am sure that there is some confusion about this. There are some riders who do look as if they are belly-dancing in the saddle, due to excessive movement of the pelvis, but this is the result of over-compensation. If the rider is taught to absorb the movement in the way that I have described, ensuring that the upper body remains erect and is not collapsing at the waist, excessive flexion never occurs, the rider doing no more and or no less than the horse's back dictates.

> In addition to the Equisimulators, I also have a mechanical simulator which works entirely by springs activated by the rider. If the rider 'rows' or 'polishes' it reacts in no uncertain manner, bottoming out on the springs to the extent that it nearly bucks her off! The rider is left in no doubt as to the heaviness of her seat when sitting to the canter in this manner.

4 LEARNING 'FEEL'

It is often said that only certain riders are born with that mystical, indefinable quality of 'feel', and that those of us lesser mortals who were not favourably endowed with it at birth will never have a hope of achieving it. I disagree. If all riders were taught, from day one, how to recognize 'feel', it would not take on the mystique that seems to surround the subject. After all, we all have nerve endings in our rear ends, so we can all feel what is going on underneath us, if we are told *how*.

True, some lucky individuals have better co-ordination than others, and this undoubtedly helps. Likewise, some people have a definite rapport with horses, both on the ground and when mounted, coupled with an innate ability to gauge the horse's personality and mood. These riders will often be exceptional, but do not despair – there is hope for all!

THE FIRST STAGE

I like to think that 'feel' can be measured in stages. The first stage in the scale of 'feel' is passive rather than interactive, with the rider learning to recognize the sequence of movement of the horse's legs underneath her, in all paces. From day one, I start to teach beginners to recognize what is going on underneath them, in walk naturally to begin with, as they do not have to concentrate on staying aboard and have time to think about what they are feeling. If beginners are started off in this way, they will learn at least the basics of 'feel', much as a child would learn the alphabet.

I remember being asked frequently by my former trainers if I could feel which hindleg was coming under, or stepping on the ground, and to my frustration I could not. It was not until I went for my first Classical lesson that I learned how to do this. The instructor asked me if I could feel which hindleg was being brought under the horse, and when the hindleg was striking the ground. When I replied that

Watch from the ground as the horse moves away from you, and observe the sideways roll of the back. See how the left hip lowers as the left hindleg is travelling under the body, and how the left side rises as the hoof strikes the ground and pushes the hip upwards and forwards. Then, once mounted, allow your pelvis to go with the movement, and feel your seatbones dip and rise with the undulations. As I have already said, thankfully the human rear end is designed in two halves, which greatly facilitates the ease with which we can learn to 'feel'!

Showing how the hindquarter lowers as the left hindleg is drawn under the body

I couldn't, he asked me whether I could feel the horse's hips dipping from side to side. He then explained that as the horse's left hip dips, that is the left hindleg being brought forward, and so my seatbone would dip on that side, and likewise to the right.

It was such a simple explanation, and I was absolutely furious to think that I had been able to feel this since learning to ride as a small child, yet nobody had told me before just how and what I should be feeling. I would gladly have paid that instructor ten times the amount for the lesson, just to learn that one thing. It was as if a key had been turned in a door, one which had been closed to me for years. Opening that door unlocked the secrets of 'feel', and an improvement in my ability to ride and school horses that I could never previously have dreamed of.

From that one simple explanation, I then was able to work out more for myself. As I knew the sequence of footfalls in all the gaits, it did not take me long to determine that if my seatbone lowers when the horse's hindleg is coming under, when I then feel my seatbone being pushed up and forward, this must be the moment when the hindfoot is pushing off the ground. I also quickly worked out that when my seatbone lowers in walk or trot, that corresponds with the shoulder coming back, and when my seatbone is being pushed up, that must correspond with the shoulder swinging forward. From there it was simple to work out how to feel the diagonals in rising trot, which we will be examining in detail later in this chapter.

Riding on the correct diagonal: rising as the outside shoulder moves forward, and sitting as the outside shoulder moves back

When you are really sure that you can feel this correctly, try also to feel the horse's belly as it moves from side to side under you. In walk, let your legs follow the swing of his belly, which will swing to the right as his left hindleg is brought under and the hip dips to the left, and to the left as his right hindleg is brought under. One of my pupils, having just learned this feeling after many years of riding and never being taught how to pick up the lateral movement of the horse's back, exclaimed that 'It's as if the horse's legs have become my own!'

4

FEELING THE DIAGONALS IN TROT

This will help you to feel the complete range of movements and be fully aware of them, and you will find this particularly useful when learning to feel the correct diagonals in rising trot. It is quite common to see riders at a high level still going off into rising trot on the wrong diagonal.

Once I had learnt to feel which hindleg was coming under and striking off the ground, it did not take long to correlate what the shoulders and belly were doing, and having worked all that out, I could very quickly go straight from walk on to the correct diagonal, without even having to go through a few strides of sitting trot.

In rising trot, the rider's seat should, of course, return to the saddle as the horse's outside shoulder is back, rising as it swings forward again. If you can feel the dip of the horse's hips, on the right rein, for example, you will feel his left hip dip as his right shoulder comes back. As you feel his left hip dip, say 'Sit' out loud at each stride. Then, as his left hip pushes your left seatbone up and forward, say 'rise': so 'sit, rise, sit, rise' and so on. If you always push up on the 'rise' beat, you will strike off on the correct diagonal.

Practising diagonals

If at first you find it difficult to feel the sideways movement of the back in sitting trot, practise your diagonals at walk. For instance, on the right rein, when you feel your left seatbone lower as the horse's back dips on that side, that is the 'sit' phase, and when your left seatbone is raised, that is the 'rise' phase. On the rise phase, practise pushing your seat up a little out of the saddle, so that it feels like a continuation of the push up of the horse's back, then return to the saddle, and so on, rising and sitting for a few strides on each rein. When you then start to practise rising at trot, it will now be much easier, as you will have the feeling already imprinted in your mind.

Most people are much more attuned to one diagonal or the other, and find it infuriating that even though they know that they should have risen one beat sooner, the seat refuses to obey the brain! Practising diagonals in walk helps to iron out this problem, because it gives you time to think and work it all out. Initially, when practising in trot, keep the pace rather slow and soft. Again, this helps to give

I gave a lesson to a BHSI a couple of years ago, who went off quite correctly on the left rein each time, but on the right rein invariably trotted off on the wrong diagonal for a few strides and then corrected it, without having to look down. I asked her why this happened: 'Oh well,' she replied, 'I always seem to know it's correct on the left rein, because it feels more comfortable, and so on the right rein, if it's wrong, it still feels comfortable, so I then change!' This is hardly the most scientific way of working it out, but I confess to having done just the same until I was taught to feel which hindleg was coming under me.

you time, and also exaggerates somewhat the sideways movement of the horse's back under you.

I believe that practising the diagonals, until striking off on the correct one is almost instinctive, is an essential basic – a step towards learning true 'feel'. Too few instructors these days seem to attach much importance to this, but I don't agree. Riding on the inside diagonal seems to 'wrong foot' many horses, particularly young ones, who are adjusting their balance to the unaccustomed encumbrance on their backs, and learning such basics prepares the rider for the feel and timing of far more advanced movements later on, such as the tempi flying changes.

TIMING THE CANTER AID

Learning to feel the movements of the hindlegs also takes the guesswork out of the timing the aids for canter. This is particularly helpful when schooling young horses, to ensure that right from the start they are encouraged and helped to strike off on the correct lead. If you can feel the outside hindleg about to come to the ground – ie as the hip lowers on that side – then you know that is the exact moment at which to give the canter aid, because it is the outside hind that instigates the first beat of canter.

THE SECOND STAGE

The second, more advanced, interactive stage of 'feel' can only come through practice, preferably riding many horses, as each one will teach you something different. True 'feel' is knowing just how much or how little of an aid to apply, the split second in which to apply it and the precise moment to release it, all performed almost imperceptibly, so that the aids are clear to the horse but invisible to the onlooker, giving a picture of harmony between horse and rider, who appear to be as one. Very few people reach this stage, not necessarily because they are incapable, but because they are rarely taught the basics of 'feel' and so learn only to ride by force, rather than subtlety (see 'Improving Feel', page 103).

When you learn to 'feel', it will bring a whole new dimension to your riding and take you on a voyage of discovery with every horse that you ride. You will find that schooling is not just a chore to be undertaken for the purpose of competing in tests; through experimenting with the aids in ever-varying combinations, and with the subtle nuances of each, it will become an end in itself. When you experience the exhilaration of teaching a horse something new and he responds with enthusiasm, because he understands the discreet and logical aids that you are applying, suddenly all the hard work and effort seems infinitely worthwhile!

LEARNING 'FEEL' – ON THE LUNGE

The best place to learn to 'feel' is on the lunge, but if your horse does not lunge safely, and/or you cannot enlist the help of a competent friend to lunge you, you can do a lot to improve your feel even when out hacking. I had to learn in this way because I had no one to lunge me, and after my first visit to Belgian Classical trainer Desi Lorent's yard it was clear to me that my riding still needed to undergo some drastic changes.

A SALUTARY LESSON

Desi had first assessed my riding, and conceded that my seat was better than he had expected, but my aids – particularly my 'b★★★★★ plebeian British hands', as he termed them – caused him to groan with despair. He put me straight on the lunge, on a small, wiry chestnut named Nimrod. I had received very few lunge lessons up to that point, and even without stirrups had always been made to sit as though I still had them, with toes up and heels rammed firmly down, my legs clamped around the

horse. Worse still, I had been made to turn my shoulders to the inside, which seemed to make me slip constantly to the outside.

On Nimrod, without stirrups or reins, I jammed my heels down as normal, clamped my lower legs on, and proceeded to perform the nearest I have ever come to an equestrian version of the 'Wall of Death' around Desi's very narrow little indoor school! The more I clung on, the faster Nimrod raced round, bucking in panic, as we reached near gallop. The centrifugal force alone on such a small circle at that speed made me feel as if I were in a spin dryer. Meanwhile, Desi, looking decidedly giddy on the end of the lunge, was loudly commanding me 'Don't grip!', which at the time did not seem to me to be sound advice.

Allowing leg to 'decontract', with toe hanging down naturally, helps to deepen thigh

Recently, I watched two ladies at the Equine Event at the British Equestrian Centre who were in the process of setting up their trade stand selling saddlery. I had to wait to drive on as they struggled to carry two life-size plastic model horses into the building. I wound down my window. 'No comments, please' said one of the ladies, grinning and puffing heavily. I couldn't resist quipping, 'Well, it's not often that you see the rider carrying the horse!' I then stopped and thought about what I had said, because were it possible to reverse the roles of mount and master, if only for a day, I think we would very soon see a vast improvement in the standard of riding.

Nearing exhaustion, after what seemed like a thousand revolutions, I finally relinquished my grip, preparing for the inevitable and merely absorbing the movement through my lower back and pelvis. As soon as I released my legs, Nimrod dropped back to trot, much to my relief, I might add. Desi immediately made me decontract my whole leg, allowing my toes to point naturally downwards. So indoctrinated had I been to turn my toes up, that Desi had to remind me repeatedly to drop them and release the whole leg downwards. This had the effect of bringing my knee deeper, and, even at the walk, after a half an hour I felt very stretched, although I was riding probably three or four horses a day at that time at home. We subsequently did a lot of work in walk, which I have since found to be the best pace in which to help pupils to stretch muscles without straining them to the point of 'feeling the burn', which is dangerous because muscle is then being torn.

The lunge is also the best place to practise learning 'feel', as you can concentrate entirely on what you are feeling without having to worry about controlling the horse. If you cannot be lunged, then think about what you are feeling when riding round the school or where you can do so safely out hacking, along quiet bridleways on a loose rein. Become aware of every movement underneath you, because, believe me, the horse is even more aware of every move you make. If a horse can feel a fly land on his back, how much more clearly can he feel you? You have the easy part; you are the rider, sitting on top. The horse has to bear the brunt of every movement that you make, so the more controlled your body becomes, the less you will move and the easier it will be for the horse to carry you.

THE AIDS – AN EXPLANATION 5

'Aid' means 'help', and it should have no lesser meaning when applied to equitation. Yet often riders give signals to the horse that are downright confusing, either because they are not sure themselves, or because they have been taught aids which, under scrutiny, do not make biomechanical sense. The unfortunate horse usually gets the blame for being difficult or stupid, when all he is trying to tell the rider is 'I don't understand'. It should go without saying that if the rider does not fully comprehend the aids that she is applying, then the horse hasn't a hope of interpreting what is being asked of him.

THE FULL RANGE OF AIDS

In this day and age, it seems that the only 'tools' you require in order to 'talk' to your horse are hands and legs. I have overheard even high-level trainers airily telling pupils who have enquired about the use of the weight and seat as aids, 'Oh, we don't bother with those nowadays', as if such practices were out of date and fit only to be relegated to the archives. How sad that this is the case, because the weight and seat enable us to apply aids which are *clear to the horse yet invisible to the onlooker.*

So what actually constitutes the aids of the weight and seat? In rising trot, we use our body weight to slow down the horse, whether to lessen the pace, if the horse is trotting too fast, or in downward transitions, to return to walk. The seatbones are used for directional purposes, so that merely by centralizing a little more weight on one seatbone or the other, the horse, feeling the change in weight distribution, tends to go to that side. By squeezing together the seat muscles and the upper thighs, we have the aid to slow down the horse or to halt. (We will be looking at the actual mechanics of these aids a little later.)

COMBINING THE AIDS

The various aids are used in combination:
- If we use only the hands and legs, we have, in effect only four 'tools' with which to control the horse, so that four, multiplied by four, gives a

maximum of only 16 combinations of aids.
- If instead, we add the use of the body weight, as in rising trot, the two seatbones for turning and assisting with bend, and the two sets of seat/thigh muscles, which we use for slowing down and to halt, we have another five tools at our disposal.
- Add to these the four others, and we have nine. Nine times nine makes 81 combinations of aids which, along with all the subtle little nuances of each, go to make up a veritable language through which we can communicate with the horse.
- Lastly, we have the voice, and the artificial aids of whip and spur – the latter two to be used as sparingly as possible.

Although I am known chiefly as a Classical trainer and remedial teacher of riding, I do not follow the paths of certain methods or aids just because this or that Classical Master advocated their use. I have misgivings about certain practices within the realms of Classical equitation: although the term has nowadays become synonymous with a more humane approach to horsemanship, you have only to look at engravings in books by the old Masters, some of whom are still held in high esteem, to see that this was not always the case. I like to think that I am taking the best from Classical equitation and combining it with modern biomechanical thinking, to create an approach that all horses and, very importantly, *riders* can grasp easily. I will also only teach what I have found actually works, the criterion for that being that the horse understands and complies willingly with my request. So many instructors just follow blindly what has gone before, regardless of the horse's reaction, without ever stopping to question whether or not something really works. My motto has become 'Listen to the horse'.

LIGHTENING THE AIDS

When riding a young horse, or an uneducated older one, the aids may need to be a little more definite in order for the horse to understand. However, as training progresses the aids should become progressively lighter, until at the highest levels they should be a mere whisper. Sadly, so often even in Grand Prix level dressage the aids are all too visible and forceful, detracting from the beauty of the discipline, which to me is primarily an art, and only secondarily a sport. It is not just the aesthetic angle that concerns me – it is the horse, who has to suffer the consequence of crude, harsh commands and brute force, because in the competition world aids of refinement are rarely taught.

All of this force is so unnecessary, and in the end counter-productive, because the horse is so much stronger than we are. To think that we can win through strength and domination is foolhardy in the extreme, and yet the horse puts up with so much.

> *A lady who is an animal therapist told me that she regularly has to treat a dressage horse for weeping sores in the corners of his mouth, which the owner sees as an acceptable part of training. Another girl, ex-head groom to a large dressage yard, said that their well-known foreign trainer kept a tube of toothpaste in his grooming kit box, to put on the (regularly) bleeding corners of his horses' mouths after schooling. I had never heard of this use for toothpaste, and cannot quite work out why it should be employed, but it was shocking to learn that anything had to be used for this purpose at all. My own vet told me that she went to treat a dressage horse for lameness and absent-mindedly ran her hand very lightly along the horse's back, whereupon he almost sat down. When she remarked on this, the owner replied, 'Oh, but that is quite normal in a dressage horse.' I do not think my vet's comments are suitable for printing here.*

THE HANDS

I will start with the hands, mainly because I believe that the mouth is the key to the rest of the horse. Uneducated hands will cause resistance in the mouth, which will set off a whole chain reaction of further resistance throughout the rest of the body. When I was a child, the highest accolade you could receive as a rider was to be told that you had 'good hands'. It is a long time since I have heard that saying, it now apparently being much more important to get your horse into an 'outline', regardless of how.

Thumb and first finger securing reins, freeing other fingers to close or open

USING THE FINGERS

I had always been taught that I must 'make a fist around the reins', closing my fingers firmly so that I could maintain a 'steady contact'. As I explained in Chapter 4, when I first went to Classical teacher Desi Lorent for help, my 'typical plebeian British hands' horrified him. I had been taught that to get the horse 'on the bit' I should saw my hands from side to side to make him drop his head. I knew instinctively that this did not feel right, but it seemed to be the accepted way of getting the horse into the ubiquitous 'outline'. Having successfully winched the head down into place, you then had to hold it there with an advised '20 pounds' of pressure in each hand.

Closing fingers in restraint, as if squeezing water out of a sponge – no backward movement of hand

Opening fingers to 'give'

At first Desi did not seem to realise that I had not been taught any other way, and despite being barracked on a daily basis for my overuse of the hand, the penny did not drop until one day in exasperation he took me aside and asked me if anyone had ever told me that I should use my fingers, not my hands, to 'ask' the horse to relax his lower jaw. If you hold the reins firmly with your thumb and first finger, you are then free to close the rest of the fingers in restraint, to vibrate the reins to ask, or to open the fingers to 'give' in reward. Nobody had ever told me such a thing.

I experimented with different horses over the next few days, and once again it was as if someone had turned a key in a door for me. I no longer felt it necessary to move my hands around, because by using my fingers there was no need. For the first time ever, subtlety of the rein aids came within my reach – and it was all so simple!

Suddenly, I no longer felt compelled to pull back my inside rein to turn or bend the horse. Instead, Desi told me to raise the inside hand – never more than an inch or two – and squeeze with the fingers as if lightly squeezing water out of a sponge. In this way, the horse will flex to the inside, just sufficiently to see his inside eye and nostril, not the whole side of his face. Lowering the outside hand, which remains in support at the base of the neck, acts as a barrier to

Top: Outside rein in support at base of neck

Right: Showing use of 'open' rein

prevent excessive bend in the neck, which causes problems that we will be discussing in Chapter 8.

With a young horse, or a less educated older one, it is quite permissible to use an 'open' rein, so that the hand is taken well out to the inside, but again never backwards. This action helps to guide the forehand around, and can gradually be reduced as the horse begins to understand.

THE BODY WEIGHT

Body weight is used to regulate the pace in rising trot, and for downward transitions from rising trot to walk. It is also used in conjunction with the seatbones during turns and circles. If the horse is running on too fast, by deliberately slowing your rise he has not so much to 'catch you up' as 'catch you down'; in other words, he slows his own tempo to keep in sync with you. In this way, it is possible to slow the pace without recourse to pulling back on the reins. Likewise, in downwards transitions to walk, instead of going down through sitting trot the

rider slows the rise until the horse drops back to walk. This has the benefit of producing a much smoother transition. It does not take many schooling sessions for the horse to become accustomed to this, and he will quickly learn to return to walk as soon as he feels you slow down your rise.

THE SEATBONES

The seatbones are conveniently shaped like rockers (see page 48) so that they permit the pelvis to flex forwards and then back to upright, enabling us to absorb the horse's movement (see Chapter 3). They also allow us to guide the horse by invisible means, because by angling the top of the pelvis slightly forwards (making sure that the torso remains upright and does not tip forwards too), we tilt the seatbone on to its front edge, placing a little more weight on

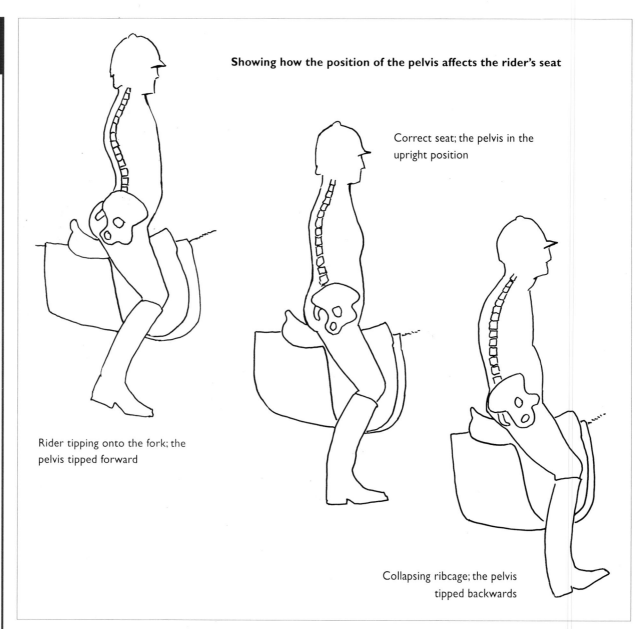

Showing how the position of the pelvis affects the rider's seat

Correct seat; the pelvis in the upright position

Rider tipping onto the fork; the pelvis tipped forward

Collapsing ribcage; the pelvis tipped backwards

it. The horse easily feels the slight change in weight distribution, and turns to that side (in Chapter 8 we will look in depth at the aids for turning).

It is easy to see, then, why it is so important for riders to sit square in the saddle. Crooked rider equals crooked horse, and if the horse is always ridden with an unequal burden it will lessen his sensitivity to the subtlety of the weight as an aid.

THE SEAT AND THIGH MUSCLES

Of all the aids, I think this is the one that those who have never discovered its use before find almost

magical. My subsequent Classical trainer, and great friend, Dr Margaret Cox taught me this use of the seat as a retarding aid. Desi Lorent had taught me the more typical Portuguese aid, which consists of bracing the spine inwards and stopping the movement of the lower back. Feeling this, the horse did respond by slowing or halting, but it seemed to me to place more weight in the saddle. You will often hear instructors telling pupils to sit more heavily through transitions, but I always thought that if I were a horse I would not be very happy if my rider suddenly sank even more weight down on to my sensitive back. I'm sure that I would respond by dropping and hollowing it, which is, of course, exactly what most horses do.

Margaret Cox taught me that by closing the buttock muscles and upper thighs we have a very effective, and totally invisible, means of slowing the horse, whether to lessen the speed of the pace, or through downward transitions, or to halt. Try this, sitting on a hard chair or stool. As you pinch your buttocks together, you will feel yourself rising upwards slightly from the chair. Your seat is not actually lifting off the chair, but the skeleton is being raised upwards by the closing and tightening of the muscles, lightening the seat in the saddle and permitting the horse's back to come up underneath

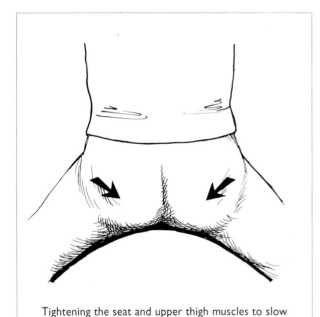

Tightening the seat and upper thigh muscles to slow the horse or effect downward transitions

you. In effect, the horse, who is accustomed to feeling your seatbones synchronizing with his movement, suddenly feels the movement arrested above him and slows accordingly.

The amount of closing of the seat/thigh muscles will vary according to the sensitivity of the horse and the stage of his training. My Arabian stallion will go from canter to halt with a strong squeeze of the seat and thighs. Slightly less, and he will go from canter to walk; less squeeze still, and he will go from canter to trot. That is just how subtle the aids of the seat can become. Some horses react more to the seat muscles than the thighs, others more to the

thighs than the seat. Most need a combination of both; it is really a question of experimentation with each horse.

It is also possible to train the horse to slow down when the rider is in the forward seat for jumping or cross-country riding, by squeezing with the lower thigh and knee, which are the only parts other than the lower leg to be in contact with the saddle.

THE LEGS

The lower legs act as the means to increase impulsion. The amount of pressure can vary from a strong squeeze to a light brush of the coat. Fellow Classical trainers often tell me that the legs should not need to have the strength of nutcrackers to ride a horse. Riders *do* need strong calves, not to grip the horse's sides like a vice but in order to have the necessary *control* of the lower leg, so that the pressure may be modulated from a brief, powerful squeeze to sharpen up a lazy horse, to a mere touch. The legs should be draped around the horse so that they are ready to be used instantly. If the calf is sticking out away from the horse, it will take a second to regain contact with the horse's sides, and that can mean missing the essential moment to time the aid to greatest effect.

The leg should be used with a slight inwards and forwards nudge of the calf muscle, not up and backwards. This latter use is ineffectual, and encourages flapping with the lower leg. The former is a much more positive signal to the horse, and is also virtually invisible.

I ask students to place a hand between my calf and the horse's side. They are always surprised that

A good dismounted exercise to help tone the calves and gain more control of the lower leg, which you can practise even while sitting in front of the television, is to obtain a large beach ball or one of those children's 'spacehopper' toys, and place it between your calves. Practise squeezing and releasing, varying the pressure of your calves, and you will soon find that you will have much greater control, and also feel and awareness when actually riding. (Do not do as one of my pupils did when purchasing a beach ball and try out all the beach balls in the shop for 'squeezability', causing a few murmurs and raised eyebrows in the process!)

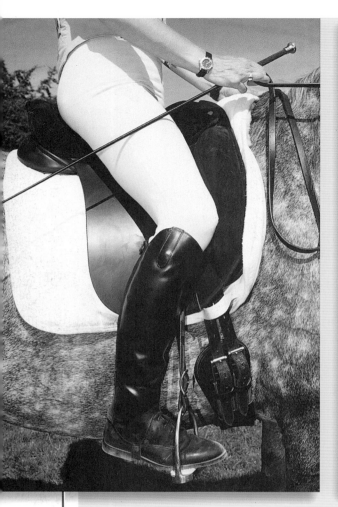

Lower leg draped around horse, ready to be used instantly (heel ideally could be slightly lower)

Calf sticking out away from horse's sides – not ready for instant use, and leg will flap when horse is moving

I can give their hand a powerful squeeze that makes them wince, yet I can also brush their fingers with the lightest touch, which can still be felt easily. Usually, when I ask students with weak and wobbly lower legs to allow me to place my hand between their calf and the horse's side, there is not enough strength there to squash a gnat!

This use of the leg is so much more effective than constantly niggling or kicking, so that the horse's sides become deadened and the rider resorts to more and more whip and spur to reinforce the leg. I have seen countless riders, particularly children on fat ponies and adults on riding school horses, kicking so hard that the thud was audible from quite a few feet away.

When giving lecture demonstrations or talks, I always get the audience to try to put themselves in the horse's place. I ask them to place the heels of their hands on their ribcage and then give their sides a good thump, not once, but a few times, and to take note of their reactions to this. There are all sorts of groans and grimaces, and I then ask the audience to stop and tell me what they felt. In every case, people tell me that they felt their ribcage 'board up', their stomach suck in, and their back muscles stiffen. I then ask them what they think horses feel when riders habitually thump away at their sides, worse still when the heel is used, and even more severely when there are spurs attached. Most people do love their horses and would not intentionally hurt them, so there are always guilty expressions to be seen around the gallery, when people are so graphically made aware.

Student placing hand between my calf and horse's side so that I can demonstrate the range of pressure and release that I use in leg aids

When using a dressage whip, bring your hand out to the side, never back, and flick the wrist so that the whip is used behind the leg. So many people use the whip with the hand in place at the wither and the horse then gets a tug in the mouth

ARTIFICIAL AIDS

It should not be forgotten that the whip and spur are termed 'artificial aids'. 'Aid' means 'to help', not 'to punish' – never use the whip or spurs negatively.

THE WHIP

The dressage whip is used just behind the leg to reinforce the aid. It can vary from no more than a flick to a sharp smack, which is the nearest that it should ever come to punishment. It can also be used at higher levels to touch the horse on the quarters, and also on the area just below the stifle on the hindleg, to increase engagement.

Take care not to catch the horse in the mouth when using a long whip. Often, I see riders jerking their hand backwards to implement the use of the whip. This is unnecessary, and is likely to provoke the very opposite to the desired reaction of increased forward movement. Instead, bring your hand out to the side and then flick your wrist, but with no backward movement, so that you can tap the horse behind your leg with ease.

Above all, the horse should not need to be afraid of the whip. When it is used with great tact, so that the touch is almost more of a tickle, it will usually galvanize the horse far more quickly than any amount of hitting, which will simply cause resentment.

SPURS

Spurs should never be used until the rider gains a high degree of control of her lower leg. They are used as the ultimate refinement of the leg aid – never in a backward, kicking manner, which would bruise or even puncture the horse's skin. Having said that, I have seen dressage riders in this country and abroad booting the horse with spurs as hard as they could, not even because the horse had 'misbehaved' in the recognized sense, but merely because he had not produced sufficient piaffe, or passage, or extension.

TAKE CARE WITH TACK

Although this chapter is about the aids, tack is, to a certain extent, either a help or a hindrance, and so almost qualifies for the term 'aid'.

BRIDLES AND BITS

I detest the current practice of having flash nosebands fitted so tightly that a piece of bandage pad or a little gel pad must be put underneath to prevent the leather cutting into the horse's nose. This, we are told, is to prevent the horse from opening his mouth and evading the bit. If someone strapped your mouth so tightly shut that you needed padding under the strap to stop it biting into your flesh, would it not provoke you into actually *wanting* to resist? To me, the whole concept is illogical.

Another practice I hate to see is that of having the bit so high in the horse's mouth that the corners of the lips are wrinkled; in fact, I have heard it advised that for the bit to be correctly fitted you should be able to see three wrinkles. Desi Lorent used to make his pupils pull up the corners of their own mouths, and then asked them how they would like to have to wear a bit in such a fashion, for at least an hour or more at a time. 'But he'll get his tongue over the bit if I don't', is usually the complaint. Occasionally, a horse will put his tongue over when the bit is lowered, but in my experience he generally soon learns not to do it. To have the bit just lying in the mouth, without pulling the lips upwards and tightening them, is infinitely preferable. Then, when he finds that he is comfortable, the horse usually learns quickly – through relaxation of the lower jaw – to accept the bit lightly and without fussing.

People often come to me for lessons bemoaning the fact that their horse will not go 'on the bit' without a fight. Apart from hard hands, one of the prime causes I encounter is the fact that many riders do up the throatlash so tightly, that as soon as the poor horse tries to flex at the poll the strap pulls up into his jowl, and practically throttles him in the process. No wonder he is reluctant to flex – it is an impossibility! Always have the width of at least four fingers, if not your whole hand, between the throatlash and the horse's cheek when he is standing at rest. In this way, when he starts to flex the strap will remain slack and will not impede his ability either to flex as required, or to breathe!

THE SADDLE

It goes without saying that your saddle should fit without impinging on the horse's shoulder movement or digging into his back muscles. Saddles are so often a source of pain and an obvious cause of evasion, bucking or rearing, frequently because riders appear to pay less attention to having them regularly reflocked or adjusted than in years gone by. With such a wide variety of numnahs and gel pads now on the market, it is more often a case of if the saddle doesn't fit, buy another new-fangled product to jack it up, often at considerably greater expense than a complete reflock with all new wool stuffing.

Lastly, do not do your girth up so tightly that the horse cannot expand his ribcage. I was appalled to see a product on the market that allows the girth to be tightened up even more than the maximum that you could pull it up by hand. At lecture demonstrations, I ask audiences once more to put themselves in the horse's place and imagine trying to go for a run

---

A friend of mine visited one prestigious national equestrian school to sit in on the schooling sessions. Within a short time, several horses' sides were holed and bleeding. To my friend's horror, two riders were actually glancing down to ensure that the spurs were placed directly into the holes. Before too much longer, the horses' flanks were dripping blood. I have seen the same happen at a regional dressage qualifier, where the winner of the Advanced Medium used her spurs so viciously that the horse's sides were bleeding as she came out of the arena. The judge made no comment.

Bit strongly wrinkling corners of mouth

Bit lying comfortably in mouth, corners still slightly wrinkled. Max has a long mouth, but comparatively short lips. Any lower, and the bit would bang his teeth

Throatlatch too tight – when the horse flexes, it will pull up into his jowl and strangle him! …

… as you can see clearly here.

Here Max is able to flex at the poll, without being throttled by the throatlatch. Ideally, I wouldn't mind seeing it even looser ...

… as Donna has here on her very chesty Lippizaner mare – she needs plenty of space to free her jowl, which hasn't a lot of room where her neck joins it

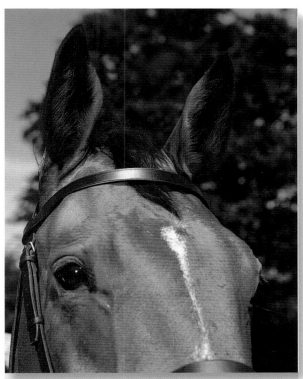

Good comfortable fit of browband – neither pinching (too tight a fit can cause head-shaking) nor too loose

around the block with their trouser belt cinched up as tightly as most riders would do up their horse's girth. Desi Lorent used always to ride with enough room in his girth to accommodate another horse! New students used to call out in alarm, 'Captain Lorent, your girth is so loose!' He would summon a working pupil and instruct them to 'Remove the girth', and would then proceed to perform everything up to and including canter pirouettes without it. 'Zere,' he would say in his broad Franco-Belgian accent, 'Zat proves it is ze balance zat keeps ze rider on board, not ze girth!'

6 THE AIDS – APPLICATION

The application of the aids is of paramount importance to the education of the horse, and yet many instructors and even trainers seem to pay only lip service to the explanation of them, and to how and why they work. If teachers have not thought about how or why something does or doesn't work, in order to be able to explain the process clearly and logically to the pupil, how can they call themselves teachers? The whole concept of *teaching* riding needs a rethink, because so many things that riders do to horses actually *cause* the very resistances and evasions that they are trying to prevent.

When, through relearning to ride in the Classical way, the confusion that I must have wreaked upon every horse I had previously ridden dawned upon me, I felt a deep sense of shame: shame that I had blindly accepted practices that now seemed blatantly unfair, in the name of 'schooling'; shame that I had not

Try a little experiment with a friend. Take a pair of reins and stand facing each other. One person gets hold of the reins at the bit end, as if he were the horse, and grasps them quite firmly, as if the horse were himself 'taking a bit of a hold'. The other person holds the reins as would the rider. The 'rider' then verbally tells the 'horse' that she is going to pull back on the reins. The 'horse' finds that his reaction is to pull back even harder, and so a tug of war ensues, much as it does on a real horse. Now, instead, the 'rider' closes the fingers of her left hand tightly on the rein, then releases the tension slightly by softening the fingers again, and alternates this process with the right hand, so that as the tension increases

(Hands on right are 'horse', on left, 'rider') 'Tug of war' situation, pulling against each other

'Rider' squeezing reins alternately (again no backward traction of hand) to encourage 'horse' to 'give'

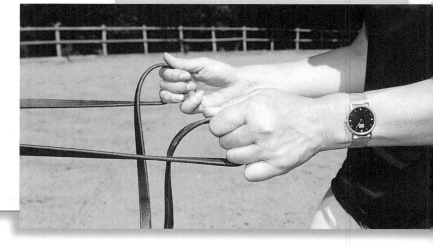

questioned the ethics of punishing a horse who was 'resisting', instead of stopping and thinking, 'What might I be doing to this horse to cause him to disobey?' Admittedly, my punishments would have been very mild in comparison with some that I have witnessed. However, to think that I had punished a horse at all for my own ineptitude filled me with an almost evangelical zeal to spread the word that there is an alternative.

THE CONTACT

I have already examined the harsh use of the rider's hands in Chapter 5. Now we will examine the cause. I truly believe that the almost fanatical belief in the use of the snaffle bit as the only bit in which to educate the horse is the prime cause of so many riders having such harsh hands. When I was a child, we rode our ponies in whichever bit they seemed comfortable. Since the emergence of dressage as a sport, those who elect to compete in this discipline are faced with a very limited choice of bits: only ten different types of snaffle, all with a basically similar action, and four varieties of bridoon and curb, the latter only permitted from Elementary level upwards.

It seems that unless you ride every horse (regardless of how much force has to be used) in a snaffle, you are treated with scorn. In days gone by, the snaffle was primarily used by grooms, whose employers did not consider they had sufficiently educated hands to ride with a double bridle. When the horse is lunged and backed correctly, being encouraged to step through and take the contact,

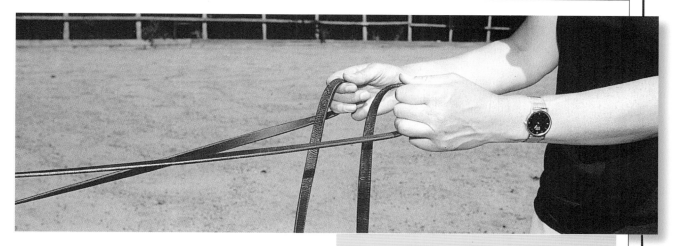

on one side, it is released on the other. The 'horse' will want to yield his hands forward towards the 'rider', much as the real horse will offer to yield his lower jaw.

As the 'horse' yields his hands forwards, the 'rider' opens her fingers (still holding the reins firmly with thumb and first finger but opening the other three) and 'gives', thereby rewarding the 'horse'. It is possible to 'give' at least a couple of inches of rein merely by opening the fingers, and likewise to shorten them by closing the fingers again, all without any need to move the hands. The 'rider' then experiments by vibrating the reins with her fingers, moving from a definite squeeze through to a mere flutter of the fingers. The 'horse' will feel even the tiniest movement of the reins through his fingers on the end of the rein, even though there is no tension, simply the weight of the reins alone. So does the real horse.

'Rider' opening fingers of right hand, releasing tension – note slackening of rein

'Rider' vibrating fingers on loose reins – 'horse' feels even the slightest fluttering of fingers on rein

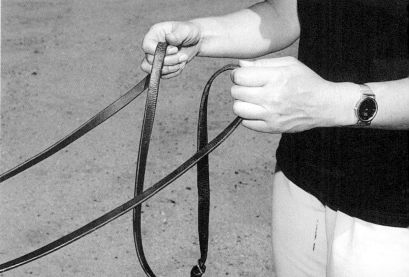

many will go kindly in a snaffle for the rest of their days, going in a double bridle as and when required for competition. Sadly, this is not often the case. Many horses are badly ridden from the start, and because the corners and bars of the mouth are covered with sensitive nerve endings, they are all too easily damaged by strong use of the hands. Many riders seem to think that the horse needs pounds of pressure maintained in each hand, or backward tugs on the reins, in order to be able to feel the rein aids. This is somewhat akin to the English habit of shouting at foreigners as if they were deaf, in the hope that they will understand!

It is this variation of tension that creates 'contact'. If a horse pulls against me, then I will close my fingers with a tension equal to that pressure, but never use my hand to pull back. Nor do I close the fingers of both hands at the same time. Again, I will use the alternating left and right squeeze as explained in the experiment above. The instant the horse yields his jaw, I open my fingers and yield the tension on the reins in reward, but at the same time close my legs a little more to keep the horse's hindlegs stepping under and the back coming up. If the horse tries to raise his head again, the process is repeated, until – often in a very short space of time – the penny drops and the horse will stay soft and relaxed in his jaw, on a very

light contact, freeing the rest of his body from the tension that prevents him from working 'through'.

THE PELHAM BIT

Although we are ridiculed by the mainstream dressage world, I and several of my Classical colleagues recommend the use of the pelham bit as the route to lightness and harmony. It is true that the snaffle is probably the only bit in which the horse will allow himself to be abused to a certain extent. In a curb bit of any variety, if you were to saw on his mouth as so many riders do in a snaffle, the horse would be very likely to stand up on end to get away from the pressure, but curb bits – pelhams or double bridles – are actually much kinder in educated hands.

The bit is the key to achieving relaxation of the horse's jaw. This is essential, because if there is stiffness and resistance in the jaw, it will set off a whole chain of tension throughout the rest of the horse. If the horse does not respond to light finger pressure in a snaffle, what is the point of having to use force, which does not actually render the jaw relaxed but instead makes the rider resort to sawing on the mouth to reel in the head at the front? When the horse relaxes his lower jaw, his head will drop down of its own accord, freeing the back to round up and enabling the hindlegs to step further under the body.

I have worked with countless horses that were supposed to be difficult to school, because they would not work 'on the bit'. In nearly every case, I have changed the bit and ridden them in a mullen mouth pelham, usually made of metal covered with rubber

Many horses do not like the nutcracker action of a jointed snaffle bit. Try placing one over your wrist, and pull back on it. Note how quickly the blood drains from your arm, leaving a white ring. Think about how this affects the horse's tongue and jaw. Twenty pounds of pressure in the hands, exerted against a jointed bit in the horse's mouth, will act like a tourniquet. One famous instructor, Commandant Jean Licart of the Cadre Noir in France, wrote that he had seen horses' tongues 'turn blue or even violet' as the result of heavy-handed riders.

Placing snaffle bit over forearm – get someone to pull back on reins. Note how skin is puckered and pinched. It hurts!

Holding double reins – snaffle rein under little finger, curb between third and little finger

Easy way to take up double reins – separate reins with snaffle rein on outside. Bring through whole hand and out under thumb, catch curb rein with third finger, then close hand around reins, securing with thumb on top

(not vulcanite, which is too hard and thick) or Kangaroo metal. The bit itself is mild, with no nutcracker action, and the curb chain acts on the curb groove, where there is a reflex point which makes the horse relax his lower jaw when light pressure is applied. With this combination, it is usually possible within seconds, and certainly within a few minutes, to achieve this merely by 'asking' with the fingers, without any force or sawing on the horse's mouth. His stride will become longer, his back will swing and, above all, he will learn to carry himself. I cannot understand the rationale of the 'powers that be', who mourn the loss of art in dressage and yet perpetuate the situation by enforcing the use of bits that encourage heavy hands. Regardless of the fact that I can often transform a previously wooden and resistant horse into one that is pliant and willing within a very short time, I have nonetheless been accused of 'cheating', because I have used a pelham bit and not the regulation snaffle. Many people say that the horse will come behind the bit in a pelham, but this is only true if you use it strongly.

The pelham must always be used with two reins, otherwise the effect is nullified. You cannot obtain

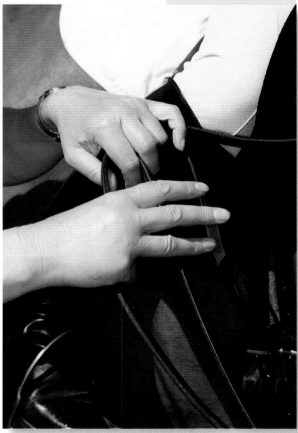

sufficient differentiation between the two actions of the bit with a single rein and roundings, which link the two bit rings. The likely outcome of using the latter is that the rider will pull back on the reins and use the bit for leverage and therefore extra brakes. This is not the intention. Being able to use the two reins acts on different parts of the mouth and the curb groove. Using one rein tends to make everything act together at the same time.

There are several legitimate ways to hold double reins, none of which are familiar to the average rider who, when confronted with two reins when riding my schoolmaster, wails 'but I've never ridden before with two reins.' I always reply that if I had five pounds for every time that a student had told me that, I would probably have the equivalent of a National Lottery win! I prefer to hold the two reins as in the photograph, with the snaffle rein under the little finger, and the curb rein between the third and little fingers. The snaffle rein should cross outside the curb rein. I am not pedantic about the way in which the reins are held, but do feel that this traditional way is the best, as the third and little fingers seem to have more flexion and dexterity than the combined use of the second and third fingers. It may just be a personal preference, but I certainly feel that I have a better connection with the horse's mouth with these two fingers.

The pelham bit is often maligned as a 'nothing' bit, that has no clear action. That is the case when roundings are used, but it is quite possible to obtain a clear action when the pelham is used in the way described in this book, so that the fingers are used to squeeze the rein, or merely to vibrate it, bringing gentle, intermittent pressure onto the reflex point in the curb groove, whereby the horse will relax and soften his jaw, without the use of any force.

I recently read a very scholarly article about the varying

leverages and compressions exerted by the pelham bit when used so that the cheek pieces of the bit are at 30, 45 or 60 degree angles from the vertical. It should never be used in that way. The bit should never come further back than at a 30 degree angle, or the horse will be forced to overbend and come behind the vertical to avoid the pain of the compression of his tongue and jaw, caused by the mouthpiece of the bit being pulled back against the corners and bars of the mouth, with the cheek pieces of the bit bringing the curb chain into action against the lower jaw.

The horse will indeed drop behind the bit to avoid the discomfort of strong pressure on the curb groove, but when the fingers are used to achieve nothing more than the relaxation of the lower jaw, the horse will lengthen, not shorten, over his topline. I could cite countless case histories of horses whose way of going I have changed in minutes by putting them in a pelham and riding in this way.

People often ask me why I use a pelham rather

In the first photograph I am riding this 14-year-old mare for the first time. This is apparently her normal way of going – tense, tight through the back and neck, and very resistant to the action of the bit, even though I am using only my fingers and not pulling back with my hand.

than a full double bridle. I find that the pelham is a good everyday bit, and is ideal for introducing a horse to the action of the curb without having to fill up its mouth with two pieces of metal. I prefer to keep the double bridle as the 'icing on the cake', the ultimate aid to refinement, to be used before and during competition.

RIDING 'BITLESS'

My own Arabian stallion, Spanish Silver, prefers not to be ridden in a bit at all. A couple of years ago he contracted a respiratory virus which left him with a strange habit. He appeared to be inspiring air over the bit, causing him to make a strangulated sound which seemed to prevent him from going freely forwards. Various tests and endoscopy have revealed nothing, but the problem continued to interfere not only with his breathing under the saddle, but also with his training. In desperation I tried him in a simple little hackamore, not the long-shanked Continental type,

but the short-cheeked English variety.

Students are surprised to see a horse that performs all lateral movements, and even early piaffe and passage, without a bit, but maintaining an outline as though he were wearing one. He is so light in the hand, and responsive to the aids of the weight, seat and leg that I can ride him in just a headcollar, as the photograph on page 65 shows. Many experts are against the use of the hackamore in any form (except that of the bosal or scawbrigg-type bitless bridles) as the improper use of the mechanical hackamore has been known to break a horse's jaw. I have ridden several horses in hackamores of the English type over the years, and found that they responded very well indeed. In every case the horse, through the activation of the chain against the curb groove, just as in the use of the pelham, relaxed the jaw and poll, and maintained a correct outline on nothing but the weight of the reins. No force was ever necessary; quite the contrary.

In the second photograph I have changed from a snaffle to a pelham, and she looks like a different horse, appearing actually to have changed shape! The tension gone, she is free to use her musculature to advantage, showing her true beauty. These photographs were taken within a few minutes of each other.

Again it all boils down to education. If the rider has rough, uneducated hands, then it goes without saying that a hackamore should not be used. A rider with such poor hands should be put back on the lunge and her seat re-educated before being allowed to handle any bit at all.

The one drawback that I have found with the current design of hackamore is that the noseband falls too far down the nose, and the curb chain often rides up above the curb groove. The horse's breathing could be severely impaired by the former, and indeed, if the horse were to strongly resist the pressure of a curb chain that had moved up the jaw, I believe that it would be possible to come up with a better design – and in fact I'm working on it!

I have found that Spanish responds almost as well in a pelham ridden only on the curb rein. He really seems to hate any feeling of snaffle action, and whilst he will work in the pelham with both reins without resisting, he is lighter than ever when ridden on only

Many Arabians have mouths that are slightly different in shape to the norm, and do not go happily in a snaffle. Often the mouth is too small to accommodate a full double bridle, and so the pelham is the answer. I have two other Arabians who go beautifully in their pelhams but hate any other bit, and I know of many of their breed who are the same. Most people seem to think that Arabians are difficult to train. They are – but only if force is used! Ridden in a pelham, using aids of refinement, the intelligence and often stunning movement of the Arabian actually makes him extremely easy to train.

Spanish Silver enjoying a canter

Spanish is perfectly happy to work without a bit at all, in an outline; I am rather forward of the vertical because I am about to ask him to stretch down 'long and low' (see below)

Here I am encouraging Spanish to take the rein down – note lowered hands to maintain a straight line from bit to elbow

Here Spanish is in a good, active working trot – on the weight of the reins

the curb (see photo on page 64). Obviously, riding on the curb alone does require very still, controlled hands.

The moral of all of this is to show that every horse is different, and should not be forced to go in a bit that he patently objects to, and which causes him to resist and evade. After all, we wouldn't like to be made to walk in a pair of shoes unsuitable for the shape of our feet, and would object in no uncertain terms at the subsequent effect on our 'way of going'! Why should the horse be any different?

THE LEGS

In the Chapter 5, we looked at the use of the legs. Now let's examine their application. We have already seen how they can be used in variation from a strong squeeze through to a mere whisper, but we will now see how they can be used with great subtlety to indicate the actual pace to the horse, in a way that means he will very quickly learn to differentiate between your intentions to walk, trot or canter, to move sideways, to change leg in canter or, ultimately, to perform piaffe and passage (see page 145).

For forward movement, the legs should be used so that the rider's toe is in line with the girth. A lot of confusion is caused by instructors telling pupils to use their legs 'at the girth'. If the calves were used at the girth, the whole lower leg would be much too far forward, putting the rider into a chair seat. Nor should the calf be used too far back. This is another common fault, which causes confusion in the horse when he is asked to perform lateral work, because the legs are being used in the 'sideways mode' all the time. Sensitive horses can be easily upset by the lower leg being used too far back, particularly if the rider also grips with the calves in an effort to stay aboard. I have seen more than one rider bite the dust as a result of backward-clutching legs! If spurs are worn the effect is compounded. Spurs should not be worn until a very stable lower leg has been achieved.

Spanish in canter – inside hind well engaged, joints really flexed, contact light, face just in front of vertical. If you pulled on the reins, I am sure he would sit down in surprise

Lower leg too far forward 'at girth'

Lower leg too far back

Rider's lower leg in correct line – ear/shoulder/hip/heel

WALK

In walk, the legs should be used in time with the swing of the horse's belly. As you feel the horse's left side dip, his left hindleg will be off the ground and stepping under. It stands to reason that the only time you can increase the engagement of the hindleg is when it is off the ground, not rooted to it. You therefore increase the pressure of your left calf as you feel the horse's left side dip and the belly swing to the right, then release the pressure of the left calf and increase the pressure of the right as the right side dips and the belly swings to the left, and so on at each stride, squeezing left, squeezing right.

When riding a horse that is idle, yes, it is necessary to use the leg most of the time at the beginning, but backed up with the whip, used behind the leg. The horse should gradually become more responsive to the leg as schooling progresses. Some very sensitive horses will need very little leg, used as stated, with a light inward and forward brush of the coat. The rider must ensure, however, that such horses are not running away from the leg and are truly stepping 'through'.

TROT

In trot, you should squeeze with both calves at the same time, once during each stride and in rhythm with the one-two tempo of the pace. On well-schooled horses who are truly 'in front of the leg' (see page 79 for an explanation of this phrase), this will be the slightest inwards brush of the calf muscles against the horse's sides. This should be all that is necessary to maintain impulsion.

In rising trot, many teachers advocate squeezing with the legs as the rider rises, but in my experience many pupils find this difficult to co-ordinate and it unbalances them – and consequently the horse. The logic behind this instruction is that the rider will be rising as the inside hindleg steps under, so using the legs at that moment will increase engagement. This is true, and I would advocate that experienced, well-balanced riders should use their legs as they rise, but for the less experienced, it is preferable to establish balance first, squeezing as you sit.

CANTER

In canter, you should again squeeze with both calves at the same time, once during each stride, but this time in rhythm with the one-two-three beat of the

pace and as you feel the back come up to its highest point under your seat. You will notice, too, that as you squeeze your calves this lifts and lightens your seat. By closing your legs at the moment that you feel the horse's back round up under you, you will lighten your seat at the same time, so assisting the lifting and rounding of the back rather than depressing it at the crucial moment.

LATERAL WORK

In lateral work, the legs are used with one predominating, asking the horse to move away from the increased pressure of that leg. Here, the leg should always be used in time with the swing of the horse's belly, increasing the pressure as it swings away and releasing as it returns. The rider's leg should never be used with a solid, unrelenting pressure at any time, least of all in lateral work: as mentioned earlier, if you have ever had a horse stand on your foot and tried to push him off, you will have found that he reacts by pushing back towards you into the pressure, squashing your foot all the more! As explained for walk, by using your leg with the swing of the belly, you will be using it at the optimum moment to increase the forwards and sideways push, as the hindleg will be off the ground and therefore in a position to be engaged.

THE SEAT MUSCLES

The aids of the seat are perhaps the most subtle of all. The action of the seat as a retarding rather than driving aid was covered in Chapter 5, but it is not used purely in downward transitions or to halt. The seat is also used as an aid to collection, so that the stride becomes more elevated and expressive, without compressing the horse into a concertina shape through strong action of the hand. For this purpose, in walk and trot, it is used unilaterally. In other words, the buttock muscles are tightened and released alternately, as the horse's hindleg pushes off the ground. It is at this moment that the back is raised underneath you on that side, and by tightening the muscle on, for instance, the left side as the horse pushes off the ground with his left hindleg, you will feel your seatbone being raised. This tightening lightens your seat on that side and allows the horse's back to raise unhindered. The aid seems to have a 'sink plunger' effect, 'sucking' the horse's back up, used always in conjunction with the lower legs, which close around the horse's ribcage. This use of the seat will encourage the horse to take shorter but higher, more expressive steps, as opposed to the short, tight steps produced when the horse is compressed between hand and leg.

THE SEATBONES

The seatbones are used as an aid to turning, and in lateral work. If the rider accentuates the weight on to the front edge of the seatbone (see page 46), the horse feels the shift in much the same way as we would if we were carrying a backpack whose contents suddenly moved to one side. In riding, we use this to our advantage, because the horse can feel the shift easily but the aid is virtually invisible to the onlooker. Even young horses feel this and learn to recognize the meaning very quickly indeed, so that any excessive use of the rein in order to turn is quite unnecessary.

We have recently backed a four-year-old Arabian filly. She has hacked out in company and alone, but I have only had time to ride her 11 times in the school. She turns with the use of just my inside seatbone and outside leg on a loose rein. Already she bends easily on both reins, halts with the seat, stays almost entirely on the bit, on a very light contact, stepping through her transitions from trot to walk and back up again, and even going straight from halt to trot. She has begun a little leg yielding, and I will shortly introduce a little shoulder-fore (early shoulder-in). This is nothing more than I would expect from any normal young horse that I have trained from the beginning. If you do not give them anything to fight, and apply aids that they can understand, progress is very rapid indeed.

LEARNING TO APPLY THE AIDS

Learning to co-ordinate the aids takes time. In one of Finnish dressage trainer Kyra Kyrklund's videos, she mentions that the Japanese have researched how many repetitions of an action a human being needs to make before it becomes automatic. Apparently, it averages around ten thousand, thoroughly reinforcing the old belief that 'Practice makes perfect'!

There is no doubt that riders born with good co-ordination find learning the aids easier than those who haven't such dexterity. My own co-ordination is somewhat lacking; when it comes to dancing, I have two left feet, and any poor fellow that risks a dance with me is liable to end up with his own feet three sizes larger! However, with practice the aids became

second nature to me, and now I rarely have to think about what I am doing when riding, even when on a strange horse with whom I need to experiment a little to find the exact amount and timing of the aids necessary for that particular horse.

There are all sorts of new-fangled techniques around that are supposed to help the rider to ride. Visualization and imaging are popular with sports psychologists, and using an endless stream of analogies seems to find favour with many instructors, some of them well known. Personally, I think that these tend to confound rather than clarify the subject for the majority of riders.

Many of the students who atttend my residential courses are so confused by being told different things by different trainers that they do not know who to believe any more. To these students I say, 'Listen to

I had one student a couple of years ago who had been taught so many analogies (none of which were actually pertinent to riding a horse) that she hadn't actually cantered her horse in the school for over a year. She had been given so many analogies and images to think of that she couldn't remember all of them, and actually apply the aids for canter as well! This really is a ridiculous situation, because it had not only confused her but had also lessened her enjoyment of riding, particularly from the schooling point of view, to the extent that she really had thought about just going back to hacking and abandoning lessons altogether.

the horse', because he will soon tell you if he doesn't like what you are doing to him, but most horses will work willingly for you if you are working with rather than against them.

The only 'visual images' I like to give students is to advise them to watch videos of the world's best riders. I always recommend Kalman de Jurenak's *Classical Schooling* videos, because Hans-Heinrich Meyer zu Ströhen, who is the demonstration rider on both, is one of the world's finest exponents of style and correct riding. Likewise, Michael Klimke, son of

Michael Klimke riding in at Goodwood in 1991

Using the fingers to encourage the horse to lower his head. Here Doric is not stepping through and his back is hollow

the great Dr Reiner Klimke, is exceptional, and to carry a mental picture of either of these when you are riding will help you to achieve the correct Classical posture and remind you to apply aids of discretion. Both riders give the impression of being totally at one with their horse and completely at ease in the saddle, and display great finesse. Even if we cannot aspire to the heights that they have reached in the competition world, establishing the correct seat and imperceptible aids will add greatly to our enjoyment and sense of achievement in riding.

RIDING SCHOOLMASTERS

It helps greatly to have a few lessons on schoolmaster horses who will give you the correct feel. On their arrival here at the start of a course, I always assess riders on one of my schoolmasters, just in walk, trot and canter, and doing simple turns and circles. Many have never ridden a horse that, for example, goes

into canter almost by their merely *thinking* the aid, and my dear old schoolmaster Butch does just this (his story appears on pages 154–5). When I ask the rider to canter on, they generally start to drive with their seat and flail their legs. 'He won't canter' is usually the complaint. When I tell the rider to sit up, sit still and *think* canter, they cannot believe it when he pops up into the pace instantly. It is always a shock to these riders to realize just how little they have to do to achieve the transition. Not all of my schoolmasters are quite as telepathic, but all will go straight into canter as long as the correct aid is applied. We will be looking at the aids for canter in more depth in Chapter 9.

EXPERIMENT!

When trying out the application of the aids, don't try to put them all together at once.

Turning

Ride in the school on a loose rein and experiment first with turning, merely by advancing your inside

Doric has relaxed his lower jaw and his head has lowered. I have released my fingers in reward and I am backing this up with use of the lower leg to engage the hindlegs. He is now really stepping through, with a swinging back, covering more ground at each stride

seatbone and centralizing a little more weight over it, and using your outside leg behind the girth, experimenting to see how much pressure your particular horse needs. Angling the inside hip in this way will also bring the outside hip back a little, enabling you to use your outside leg behind the girth with ease, without drawing up your heel. We will be looking at the mechanics of this in Chapter 8.

Flexion

Experiment with achieving flexion in the horse's lower jaw by using your fingers as described on pages 58–9, encouraging the horse to lower his head. Release and reward when this happens, but at the same time send the horse forward in walk, using your legs with the swing of his belly to encourage a longer and more ground-covering stride, with the horse really overtracking and stepping through from behind (for an explanation of these terms, see page 80). Practise also flexing the horse to the inside with the fingers of your inside hand, just enough to see his inside eye, at the same time lowering your

outside hand against the base of the horse's neck in support.

Using the seat and body weight

On a light contact, try out the aids of the seat and thigh muscles. If you are riding on a very forward-cut GP/jumping saddle, it may be necessary to quit your stirrups to begin with, dropping your thigh and knee down. This is because if your thighs and knees are angled upwards, you will not be able to achieve the 'pinch' of the upper thigh, which is normally necessary to begin with to enable the horse to understand. As the horse becomes more and more familiar with the aids of the seat, you will find that he will answer to just a closing of the seat muscles alone. When you are standing up in your stirrups for fast work, or in the forward seat when jumping, he will

A few lessons on a schoolmaster can be beneficial. Here, a working pupil at Suzanne's Riding School rides Doric

learn to slow to a closing of your lower thigh, down to the knee.

■ First, try walk to halt, then trot to walk. In the latter, you may overdo the 'squeeze' to start off with and find that your horse has halted completely! If this happens, simply reduce the squeeze, experimenting to find just the right balance to ask the horse to walk, not halt.

■ Next, try out the use of the body weight in rising trot, to maintain and/or regulate tempo, and also in downward transitions. This has the advantage of being much easier for a novice rider to achieve than attempting to go through sitting trot to walk, when the usual result is bouncing in the saddle and a hefty jolt in the mouth, making life very uncomfortable for the horse.

I remember clearly how difficult I found it to use more than just my hands and legs after so many years of riding in that way. After my first visit to Desi Lorent's school, I went home not altogether convinced. I knew that I wanted to learn a different way to ride, but I was sure that it would take months, even years, for me to reschool all my horses, which from a business point of view would not have been economically viable.

Over the following week, I rode every horse or pony on the place, liveries and my own, that was big enough to carry me. To my delight and astonishment, every single one reacted as if they had been schooled in this way all their lives. I almost felt them breathe a sigh of relief as if to say, 'Thank God, she's learned to ride at last!' Naturally, I still had a lot to learn, but just by experimenting in the way outlined above, practising combining just two of the aids at a time, each horse responded instantly. It occurred to me at that point that at last I was working with, not against the horse, utilizing reflex points and simple laws of physics to create a universal language that all horses understand. It was so exciting! Over the years I have ridden literally hundreds of horses in this way, and it still never fails to delight me that they respond every time.

UNDERSTANDING SCHOOLING TERMS

I have included this chapter because I find that many riders are being taught using the standard schooling terms and phrases, without ever being given a clear explanation of what they actually mean! Phrases such as 'on the bit', 'in front of the leg', 'ride inside leg to outside hand', 'support with the outside rein' and so on are quite meaningless unless the instructor actually clarifies the concept of each one. Only last week, I taught a new pupil who is riding at Medium level

Dianne Breeze on Ebe, demonstrating what can be achieved through concentrated effort and determination

dressage. She said that her instructor was very keen on the term 'inside leg to outside hand', so I asked her what it actually meant to her. She hadn't a clue! This is a regular occurrence with pupils at all levels. It never ceases to amaze me how little riders really do understand about the technical side of riding.

I enjoy going to the village cricket match in the summer, mainly because it actually stops me working for a few hours and I get a chance to relax with friends. When I first started spectating, I thought that I would never even begin to understand the complexities of the game, but thanks to clear, concise explanations from several male friends who play, I am now relatively *au fait* with at least the more common cricketing terms. While listening to them, it struck me just how well the players of this and most other sports understand these terms and phrases, in comparison with the average rider's comprehension of the equivalent in equitation.

ON THE BIT

Let's start with 'on the bit'. The FEI dressage rules describe it thus:

A horse is said to be 'on the bit' when the hocks are correctly placed, the neck is more or less raised and arched according to the stage of training and the extension or collection of the pace, and he accepts the bridle with a light and soft contact and submissiveness throughout. The head should remain in a steady position, as a rule slightly in front of the vertical, with a supple poll as the highest point of the neck, and no resistance should be offered to the rider.

If you look at the majority of horses in the dressage arena today, you will see that this is rarely the case. Most have their heads behind the vertical, with the neck above the third vertebra rather than the poll being the highest point. The contact is neither light nor soft, and the horse looks tense and resistant, not submissive. What is the point of making rules, if few actually take any notice of them? For competition dressage, this rule needs to be clarified. Does it still stand, in its present form, or should it be changed to permit this 'new' way of going?

For me, the old rule is still relevant, but perhaps with one allowing factor. Modern sporthorses, and many stallions, have crestier necks than the majority of dressage horses of a few decades ago, when the rules were written. Looking at old archive film, and photographs in books written in that era, it is quite clear that the musculature and general shape of dressage horses then and now is very different. Modern horses are much more developed over the topline, and to ask many of them to bring the poll up as the highest point would actually cause them to hollow behind the wither and drop the back, rather than raise and round it. While watching a recent performance by the Spanish Riding School, it was interesting to note that very few of the stallions had the poll as the highest point. I have spoken to several world-renowned trainers about this, and all are agreed that it is acceptable for a horse to have the third vertebra region of the neck as the highest point, providing that the face does not come behind the vertical.

DO *NOT* USE FORCE

The state of being 'on the bit' is a combination of several factors. It is not just a question of getting the horse's head down. In Chapter 6, we have looked at the issue of 'contact' and the relaxation of the horse's lower jaw. I would like to see those words incorporated into the FEI rule, because the first requirement is for the horse to accept the bit, taking a light, soft contact without resistance. If the rider attempts to get the horse on the bit by force – by sawing on the reins and reeling in the head, only to have to hold it there with arms like high-tensile steel – of course it will set up resistance and evasion, because such actions create discomfort.

If a human being finds something uncomfortable, they are usually in a position to do something about it. If we are wearing shoes that hurt, or our trouser belt is fastened too tightly, then we simply change the shoes or loosen the belt. If a person is sick or otherwise unable to do this for herself, at least she can usually tell another person that she is uncomfortable.

When riders are taught to use force, it stands to reason that the horse will be uncomfortable. A few months ago, a lady sent me a video of her schooling at home. The horse, an attractive Danish Warmblood, was very tense and stiff through the back and contracted in the neck, and was being held in a vice-like grip by his rider. She was trained by a Continental Grand Prix level rider, who had told her that she needed to hold her horse in more at the front. She had replied that she was already using all her strength to hold him where he was. To my astonishment, her trainer had then advised her to start weight training in order to achieve more strength in her arms, so that she would then find it easier to keep her horse 'on the bit'!

The horse cannot communicate with language: he has to tell us in another way, which is often misinterpreted as bad behaviour.

When 'on the bit', the horse should look relaxed and happy, his mouth should be wet and he should hold the bit lightly, without constantly champing it. His neck should look soft and unrestrained, even at advanced levels, when although the neck will be raised and arched proudly, it should never look as though it is being forced into that position, with muscles bulging and veins standing out. In fact, the neck should look as it would if the horse were prancing in a field, showing off to his companions. His back should be soft and swinging, his hindlegs engaged according to his stage of training, so that the body, neck and head appear to connect as a whole and not to be working in three separate pieces, as will often happen when force is used.

RELATED TERMS

At this point we need to examine the terms 'above the bit' and 'behind the bit', and 'on the forehand'.

- 'Above the bit' means just that – the horse has raised his head and poked out his nose, which will

Horse accepting bit, contact light but positive. Horse's expression happy. This mare has a crest like a stallion – for her to have her poll as the highest point, she would have to disengage her back behind the wither

make him hollow his back and trail his hocks out behind.

■ 'Behind the bit' means that the horse does not take the contact, dropping the bit and often opening his mouth, and bringing his nose well behind the vertical, sometimes almost to the point where it is touching his chest; horses that have been ridden in draw reins have a tendency to do this.

Horses that go 'behind the bit' will be just as unable to engage their hindlegs as those that go 'above the bit', and both are equally 'on the forehand'. Many riders find this a little difficult to understand: a horse that feels heavy and leans on your hand would naturally seem to be weighting his front end, while the horse that raises his head would seem

'Lady' is a 12-year-old ex-point to pointer, and had never before received any schooling. Riding her for the first time, after a few minutes she understood, relaxed her jaw, and started to swing through her back with wonderful rhythm and impulsion, on a very light contact. Her owner looked amazed, at the transformation from nose-poking racehorse into rather nice potential dressage horse! She drove up to see me the following day. 'I so enjoyed watching you ride Lady yesterday', she said, 'she looked like butter in your hands.' That, to me, sums up what it should feel like to ride a horse 'on the bit'. The yielding of the lower jaw releases the whole body from tension, enabling the rider to 'mould' the horse, like butter, so that his movement flows, whatever the pace or exercise.

Above the bit – horse has raised head, dropped back

to be relieving the forehand of weight. In truth, by raising his head the horse disengages his back behind the wither, again trailing his hindlegs out behind him.

In either case, the horse ends up pulling himself along by his front legs, much as a carthorse puts his shoulders into the collar to pull a heavy weight, instead of propelling himself forward with his hindlegs by stepping further under his body and flexing his hind joints. The process of schooling encourages the horse to take the weight further back, adjusting his centre of gravity, so that the hindlegs provide the power and impulsion, and the shoulders are free to lift and lighten, increasing the life and expression of the movement.

IN FRONT OF THE LEG

Dressage riders often state that the horse must be 'in front of the leg'. This can seem a rather peculiar expression but, properly explained, it makes sense for the rider. I am sure that the current propensity for hurried dressage, which is all about power and speed, as opposed to the stately, collected work to be seen in the great Classical schools of Europe, has something to do with this term. It does seem to imply to many that the horse has to be scuttling along, almost as if he is ahead of the rider. The real meaning is much more simple altogether.

'In front of the leg' means that the horse should respond immediately to the rider's leg aids, at that moment, and not five or ten seconds later. This does not mean that the horse should be so sharp that he is

Behind the bit – in this case, horse has dropped the bit and come behind the vertical and is not connecting through from behind

not so much responding to as running away from the leg, but that he learns that the legs mean 'step under', not 'go faster' (see page 81).

TRACKING UP

'Tracking up', is another widely used schooling expression which has a very simple meaning: the horse is said to be 'tracking up' when his hind feet fall into the hoofprints of his forefeet. This can be seen clearly in the surface of the school. If the horse is not tracking up, his hind hoofprints will be some way behind those of his forefeet. If the horse is crooked (a subject we shall be looking at closely in Chapters 8 and 11), then the imprints of his hind feet will be to the left and right, or right and left, of those of the forefeet, depending on which side he is stiff. 'Overtracking', as we would like to see in the walk when the horse is taking long, free strides, is where the imprints of the hind feet actually come in front of those of the forefeet by anything up to, or even exceeding, 30cm (12in).

Tracking up seems to have almost too much significance attached to it in current dressage training, and is the prime cause of trying to run the young horse too fast, ahead of his own natural rhythm. A youngster, or an older horse being reschooled, will be unable to maintain the spring and cadence in his stride if forced to track up. Only when the horse strengthens and develops more power, can he be asked for more pace, and he will then be able to track up with ease.

Likewise, a horse in collection will seldom track up. The hindlegs must step under, but only to the degree that permits the compression of the joints that produces the spring and upward elevation of collection. If the hind feet are too far underneath the horse's body, there is a danger of the weight being transferred back to the shoulders – rocking-horse fashion – because the horse cannot maintain his balance, and the joints, although flexed, will be unable to compress to provide the upward impetus to the stride.

THE OUTSIDE REIN

'Ride inside leg to outside hand' and 'support with the outside rein' are inextricably entwined. You have to know the meaning of the latter in order to be able to do the former! I often used to wonder what 'support with the outside hand' meant. The phrase itself doesn't really tell you much at all, but seems to imply that you either hold the horse's front end up with it – in which

'Tracking up', when the hind feet fall into the prints of the forefeet; a sign that the horse is strengthening and developing power

Desi Lorent taught me how to ride, but it was my subsequent trainer, Margaret Cox, who opened the door to the training of the horse and what to 'feel' for at each stage of training. Margaret lives a hundred and fifty miles away, and when she first began to teach me she would give me lessons over a whole weekend on various horses, and then leave me with enough to consolidate until her next visit. After one weekend, I worked on my Arabian stallion, then at a fairly early stage in his training, to get him going more forward, as I was convinced that he wasn't stepping under and tracking up. I did lots of transitions to get his hocks further under him, but he still felt as if he needed to go faster.

I asked my yard manager to video me riding the stallion. To my surprise, I realized that he was indeed tracking up and stepping under, and looked light and mobile in his shoulders. I had been fooled because he has such good flexion in his hind joints and a natural ability to step under, without needing to increase his speed, and all I had been doing was running him out of his own natural rhythm and flattening what came naturally to him! I telephoned Margaret, who explained that when the horse starts to step under and really flex his hocks, the rider will become less aware of the hindlegs working, but will feel more sensation of the shoulders lifting and lightening, as if you have more horse in front of you than behind. For me, this – combined with the feeling of the horse responding immediately to the leg – succinctly sums up the meaning of 'in front of the leg'.

case I would suggest that a crane might better be employed – or that it helps prevent the horse from leaning over sideways! Rarely does anyone explain to the rider exactly *how* the outside rein is used.

The outside rein is used to assist the horse in a turn or circle, or to achieve the displacement of the forehand to the inside, as in lateral movements. We will be looking at its use in relation to these in greater depth in Chapters 8 and 11. To do this, the hand should be lowered and held just touching the horse's neck, so that the rein lies along the length of the neck.

■ Acting passively, with the rein pressed lightly against the neck, it forms a kind of barrier which tells the horse, 'Don't drift through your outside shoulder'. It also limits the bend, so that the horse doesn't jack-knife at the base of his neck.

■ Applied with a little vibration against the neck, the rein says to the horse, 'Move your forehand over', as in shoulder-in, travers and other lateral movements.

All horses quickly learn to respond to the action of the outside rein, easily distinguishing between the passive action of its use as a barrier and the active, vibrating mode used to achieve the displacement of the forehand. In fact, most horses will catch on to the idea within the first lesson.

In my yard, the young horses are led from stables to field (we do not have to go on roads) with just a lead rein around their necks. To stop or slow down, we apply pressure around the base of the front of the neck by drawing the rein backwards. To turn left, the

rein is brought out to the left; to turn right, the hand is passed under the neck and brings the rein out to the right. From the moment they are backed, our young horses therefore understand the use of the outside rein. Teaching them to turn under saddle then presents no problems at all.

'Ride inside leg to outside hand' has for me perhaps two interpretations. It is used when talking about the use of diagonal aids to straighten the horse, but also when turning or circling, or when performing leg yielding or shoulder-in. The full meaning of the phrase is explained for each circumstance in Chapters 8 and 11. Another phrase in the same category is 'falling through the outside shoulder', meaning that the horse drifts outwards on bends and circles, rather like a car with understeer. Again, this term is best explained within the context of turns and circles, and you will find details in Chapter 8.

IMPULSION

You will often hear the term 'impulsion' used in equestrian parlance. Impulsion is the energy within the horse, created by the rider's legs, which encourage him to step further under his body. Impulsion is often confused with speed, particularly in modern dressage. I watched this year's European Dressage Championships on satellite television, and was disappointed to see how many tests seemed to be completed in two-thirds of the allotted time, so hurried and tense was the work. It is forward, forward, forward these days, and all about power, speed and the extravagant extensions, which

Recently I attended a clinic taken by Kalman de Jurenak, the well-known Hungarian trainer. A very impressive horse came into the school, ridden by his trainer, who proceeded to trot the horse around in a very hurried fashion. I could see that by slowing the horse down, the movement would actually be doubled in amplitude. Just as I was thinking this, Kalman called out to the rider, 'Slow everything down! This horse has enough impulsion for three horses, in fact he could have lent some to several of the horses this morning!' As soon as his rider slowed the tempo, the magnificent power and natural rhythm of the horse became evident. His hocks stepped under like Z bends, lifting and freeing his shoulders, and in turn giving more expression to the whole stride. It did not take a lot of imagination to picture this horse, a Warmblood, three or four years hence, producing some stunning piaffe.

A few months ago, I was teaching a new pupil on her young Arabian gelding. Her previous trainer had persuaded her that it was necessary to have the little chap buzzing round the arena like a sewing machine. Unless he was going twenty to the dozen, his rider did not think that he could be tracking up or have sufficient impulsion. I got on and rode him, slowing everything down but increasing the swing and step under, working him long and low. Five minutes later he was covering twice the distance, back swinging and soft, in half the number of strides. I put his owner back up and showed her how to achieve the same. She managed this rather well, and I was very pleased, but then she seemed unhappy because she felt that her horse couldn't possibly be working 'through' from behind at what seemed to her such a low speed. I replied that he was tracking up easily, so what more did she want? He certainly hadn't been before, when he had been going at twice the speed!

show off the purpose-bred paces of the modern dressage horse. It is a rarity indeed today to see a really good piaffe or pirouette in competition dressage, not just because these horses are geared more towards extension than collection, but also because the training has veered away from the Classical and shortcuts are being taken to produce horses to Grand Prix level in a shorter time.

COLLECTION AND EXTENSION

'Collection' is another term open to misinterpretation. In dressage circles it is often misconstrued by riders who seem to think that it simply means shortening the steps. This is usually achieved by pulling in the front end and pushing the horse up from behind, until he is concertinaed between hand and leg. The resulting stride is certainly shortened, but lacks the engagement of the hindquarters and the elevation and spring that is the hallmark of true collection.

I like to think of collection as storing energy, rather as you would build up steam in a steam engine. Instead of imprisoning the horse between hand and leg to achieve the shortening, the energy is contained by the seat and fingers, and is directed upwards, increasing the spring in the joints and producing the necessary lightness of footfall.

I also liken the seat and fingers to the steam engine's valves. By opening or closing the valves, you

can release or contain the steam. Likewise, by opening or closing the seat and fingers they act in the same way as 'valves', releasing or containing the energy created by the rider's legs. We will be looking at collection in more depth in Chapter 9.

'Extension' is the opposite of collection, where the horse covers more rather than less ground with each stride. Extended paces can only truly be performed correctly when the horse has developed some

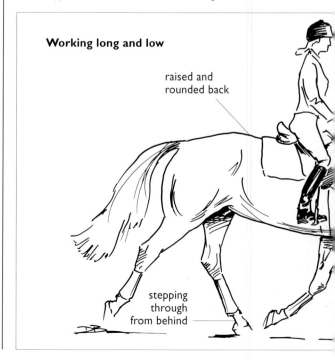

Working long and low

raised and rounded back

stepping through from behind

collection. Too often, extended trot passes muster when it shouldn't, merely because the horse has flashy, extravagant paces and finds it easy to fling his legs out in front of him, flicking his toes. Frequently, the horse quickens as he goes to lengthen, resulting in a flattened elongation of his body. In the extension, the horse should not quicken his rhythm when lengthening his stride, but merely cover more ground with the tempo remaining the same. Instead of flattening, the horse should raise and lighten the forehand, giving an appearance of riding uphill, and should step very well under behind, so that the movement comes from the shoulders rather than by flicking out at the knee.

'LONG AND LOW' VERSUS 'WORKING DEEP'

There is some controversy and confusion surrounding the modern schooling techniques termed 'Long and low' and 'Working deep', because not everyone realizes that there is a real difference between the two.

In 'long and low', we have the useful warming-up and stretching regime, rather like a ballet dancer doing exercises at the barre. 'Long and low' is also used at intervals throughout a schooling session to give the horse a break and allow him to stretch his neck and back, particularly as a release from the collected work. It is important to ensure that the horse is not simply lowering his head and mooching along in a ridden version of the grazing position, but is truly stepping through from behind, raising and rounding his back, and lowering his head and neck as a result. As you ask the horse to stretch down keep the hindlegs stepping under by closing your lower legs around him. Ask for relaxation of the lower jaw with the fingers as described in Chapter 6, then open the fingers and lower the hands either side of the wither and allow the reins to slip through the fingers as the horse takes the rein down. You should be able to feel his back rounded up under you, undulating softly. If the horse's back feels stiff and plank-like under you, he is not working 'through'.

'Through' is another term much used in dressage nowadays, and one which needs to be explained before we turn to the subject of 'working deep'. The horse is said to be 'through' when he is allowing the rider's aids to be applied without resistance, his hindlegs are stepping well under his body mass, his back is raised and free, his shoulders are light and mobile, and his head and neck are placed according to his level of training, accepting a light, elastic contact.

'Working deep' is a system whereby the horse is worked with his head lowered and face well behind the vertical, sometimes to the extent that his chin is nearly touching his chest. The method was most famously used by Olympic rider Nicole Uphoff for her brilliant Olympic gold medal horse Rembrandt. He was notoriously spooky in the arena, particularly

Working deep

neck stretched and lowered

lower jaw relaxed

face behind the vertical, head lowered

Taking the rein down long and low (in just a headcollar – who says pure-bred Arabs can't lower their heads!)

in his earlier years, sometimes even to the point of costing him the competition. With Rembrandt, working him with his head between his knees when warming up at a competition meant than when he entered the arena he would bring his head up to where it should be, rather than above the bit and therefore well placed to spook. Rembrandt was an exceptional athlete, and Nicole is an exceptional rider. She still uses the system for her other horses, with great success, but she is able to bring the horse back up through her considerable feel and skill. Others have copied the idea, but few have been able to prevent their horses becoming overbent and well behind the vertical at all times.

Dr Reiner Klimke, the great German dressage maestro, has always been outspoken against the technique of 'working deep'. He feels that the rider has to encourage the horse to step *too* far under the body, so that the back peaks up into a bow, causing the head and neck to curl back. This keeps the horse in a more horizontal rather than an uphill plane, which he believes is detrimental to true collection, as it does not encourage the horse to take the weight back and increase the flexion of the hind joints. I would tend to agree with this view, as I feel that

'Working deep', although not an extreme example – pony's face is behind vertical, and third vertebra region of neck clearly the highest point

riders who do not fully understand the technique are in danger of doing their horse more harm than good.

This is particularly so when the rider resorts to using draw reins or other gadgets to pull the horse's head down and in. There is also a tendency for riders to keep their horses in the 'long and low', or 'deep' positions for too long. Speaking at a clinic he took in England a couple of years ago, Dr Klimke said, 'You British still have your horses working long and low when they are ten years old!' – meaning that it is merely a tool to encourage the horse to stretch, not the be-all and end-all of training.

When the rider has a good grasp of the meaning of schooling terms, she is better equipped to learn. Many instructors do not take the time and trouble to explain in a clear and logical way precisely what each phrase means, so the pupil – often too overawed to ask – remains ignorant of the facts, gleaning snippets here and there from books, but possibly misinterpreting some things along the way. This can lead only to confusion, not just for the rider but also for the horse, and this in turn creates discord rather than harmony in their partnership.

Turns and circles are an essential ingredient in the successful schooling of the horse. By executing these exercises, we both supple and straighten him. However, simple as they may sound, riding a good turn or circle is not as easy as it may at first seem.

CROOKEDNESS

Most horses are born crooked, and find it easier to bend on one rein than the other. They also tend to favour one leg, much as humans are left- or right-handed. If you observe young horses at play in the field, they will often tend to lead more with one leg than the other. On the other hand, they will neatly execute a flying change of leg in order to preserve balance, as and when they need to.

It is said that horses are born with their muscles longer on one side of the body than the other – hence their ability to bend to one side more easily than the other, and also the crookedness which arises when working on straight lines. It is often overlooked that the least favoured hindleg is weaker than the other, and is therefore unable to produce equal thrust as the foot pushes off the ground. In fact, it is quite easy to spot the weaker hindleg, because when viewed from behind the hock – and even the fetlock – it will tend to 'screw' outwards. All these factors present a problem when asking the horse to perform turns and circles.

If the left hindleg is the weaker one, when on a right bend the stronger right hindleg will tend to push the quarters out to the left, because the left hind cannot match the thrust of the stronger leg. Likewise, on a left bend, the stronger right leg can push the quarters slightly inwards. You can clearly see this happening, as the stronger hind will tend to cross over the weaker one, instead of landing in the hoofprint of the foreleg on that (the stronger) side, as it will when the horse is suppled and straightened. It can also take a split second longer for the weaker hindleg to travel under, because the hock screws outwards rather than moving directly under, as will the hock on the stronger leg. This can lead to some inequality in the gait, producing very slight unlevelness. However, as schooling progresses and the weaker leg strengthens this will even out.

TURNING CORRECTLY

In order to turn correctly, the horse must bend evenly from poll to tail. The inside hindleg must step under, into the track of the inside foreleg, lowering the quarters on that side. The bend continues to a small degree through the ribcage and on from behind the shoulder, the neck bending no more than the rest of the curve, so that the rider can see no more than the horse's inside eye and nostril – *not* the whole of the side of his face.

Obviously, with youngsters or unschooled older horses, the larger the diameter of the turn or circle, the easier it is for the horse to execute. By gradually suppling and stretching, we can ask the horse to make smaller and smaller circles, culminating at the highest levels in canter pirouettes, where the horse describes a circle of a diameter little more than his own length.

AIDS FOR TURNING

The usual aids to turn consist of:

- Asking the horse to bend with the inside rein, the outside hand in support but 'allowing' the bend
- Turning the shoulders to the inside
- Holding the inside leg at the girth to maintain impulsion
- Placing the outside leg one hand's width behind the girth, to control the quarters and prevent them from escaping outwards.

Julian Marczak, co-proprietor and chief instructor of Suzanne's Riding School, riding his Andalucian stallion Emperador, showing the deeper bend executed by an advanced horse

TURNING THE SHOULDERS

Usually, great emphasis is placed on the turning of the rider's shoulders: when I was teaching BHS students, years before I turned to Classical training, we wanted them to turn their shoulders to the extent that the teacher, standing in the centre, was able to see any logo on the front of their sweatshirts.

We are taught that by turning the shoulders we are keeping them parallel with the horse's shoulders. Where (rarely) the weight aid is taught, we are told to advance the inside hip so that our hips are also parallel with those of the horse. In reality, this doesn't happen!

If you observe a horse moving around a corner or circle, does he move only his outside shoulder and inside hip forwards? No: his inside shoulder moves forwards, then his outside shoulder, and so on, and likewise his hips. In that case, if we are truly to be parallel with the horse's shoulders and hips, we should all be moving our shoulders left then right, left, right, and hips oppositely right, left, right, left. It seems to have escaped the notice of trainers that we do not actually sit on either the shoulders or hips of the horse, but in between the two! Because of this, thinking about keeping parallel with the horse's shoulders and hips is irrelevant. It is the slight shift in weight that the horse feels, and we use this to our advantage as a very subtle and almost invisible aid.

By advancing the inside hip – tipping the pelvis slightly forward on that side and thereby centralizing a little more weight on to the inside seatbone – the rider initiates the turn. All horses are sensitive to weight, and the more you practise the weight aids, the more sensitized the horse becomes to them.

Try sitting on a hard stool, so that you can clearly feel your seatbones under you, and experimenting. Turn your shoulders right, and feel where your weight goes – this will be on to the left seatbone. Your outside (left) hip will slide forward slightly in the process.

Now, tip the top of your pelvis to the right, almost as if you were pointing your hipbone into the direction of the turn and feel the weight move on to the front edge of the right seatbone. You will also be aware that your left hip has moved slightly back.

When the inside hip is advanced, the outside shoulder is drawn very slightly back, probably no more than an inch. Bringing the outside shoulder forward can have consequences that we will examine in a moment.

As mentioned in Chapter 2, we are often told that when riding we should mirror as closely as possible what we would naturally do on the ground. When you are walking and make a turn, say, to the right, do you consciously turn your shoulders to the inside, bringing your left shoulder forward? In fact, in order to turn you will advance your right leg and hip, and as you do so your left shoulder will move very slightly back. If you turn your shoulders to the inside when mounted on a horse, you will feel your weight slip to your *outside* seatbone, not the inside.

In order to use your outside leg behind the girth, with the weight into the heel, your outside hip needs to be back, not forward. Therefore, advancing the inside hip not only initiates the turn, but also allows the outside leg to be used behind the girth with ease. When the outside hip slips forward, as it will if you turn the shoulders, it is difficult to use the outside leg effectively without drawing up the heel, thereby weakening the whole aid.

DRIFTING OUT AND LEANING IN

One of the most common problems to be found when riding turns or circles is that the horse 'falls through his outside shoulder'. For example, on a right bend, the horse turns right but drifts left, making the bend or circle larger in the process. Unfortunately, it is the very act of turning the shoulders that causes this to happen: when the outside shoulder is brought forward, the weight slips to that side and directs the horse towards it. Often, turning the shoulders to the inside also results in the inside hand pulling back. This will make the horse bend at the base of the neck, so that he 'jack-knifes' and has no option but to drift outwards, particularly if the outside hand has moved forward and is permitting an excessive bend in the neck. The bend should come from behind the wither, not in front of it.

If you view the horse from the ground, you will notice that as he drifts outwards, his forelegs will be leaning inwards at an angle to the ground. Each time the inside foreleg hits the ground at an angle, it will 'prop' the horse outwards through the shoulder. If the horse is correctly bent, stepping well under with his

Horse drifting through outside shoulder, neck 'jack-knifing' to inside – bend not consistent from poll to tail

inside hindleg and thereby freeing and raising the inside shoulder, his legs should remain perpendicular to the ground. To my astonishment, I have heard trainers actually teaching that the horse should lean in on bends and circles, even advocating that the rider should also lean slightly inwards, so that he or she remains at the same angle to the horse! Quite apart from the fact that this is incorrect, it can also be

dangerous. I have seen more than a few horses tip up on slippery going because they are leaning inwards: the inside foreleg, being at an angle to the ground, slips away from under the horse and he topples over, often pinning the rider underneath and resulting in a nasty accident.

LOGICAL AIDS

There are many people who will disagree with me for teaching the aids that I recommend, in fact many teachers and trainers will think that it is nothing short

Some years ago, before I started to train Classically, I had a good working student who was training with us for her BHS exams. We had a real problem trying to teach her to rotate her upper body into the turn, as was required for her to pass her exam. Strangely – as it seemed at the time – none of the horses 'fell through their outside shoulders' with her. Although she was supposedly riding the turn wrongly, it seemed that the horses were all doing it correctly. I found this quite mystifying. The student failed her examination twice because of this, so in desperation I took her to a Chief Examiner, with whom we spent two full afternoons. We both racked our brains to think of ways to try to make her turn her shoulders, and by the end we had somehow succeeded – I can't even remember how!

Immediately, I noticed the horses that she rode then started to drift through their shoulders. It appeared that now my student was turning 'correctly', the horses were all doing it wrongly! I also observed that she was having to use more outside leg and hand to hold the horse into the turn in order to correct the drift, whereas before she had appeared to do almost nothing except naturally to advance her inside hip, bringing her outside shoulder marginally back. It was not until I went to Desi Lorent, who actually taught me to do this, that it dawned on me what had been happening. I had been trying to change what had been natural to my student and was, in fact, biomechanically correct. She passed her exam, but from that day had trouble preventing horses from 'falling through the outside shoulder'. I could have kicked myself for spoiling her instinctive use of the weight, but at the time I knew no better.

of sacrilege! However, I tried the method of turning the horse by turning my shoulders for many years, prior to retraining with Desi Lorent, who taught me the aids that I have always used since, *purely because I have found that they work* – on every horse I have ridden from that time on. When you evaluate the facts that I have already set out, you will see that, biomechanically, these aids make sense.

Desi Lorent taught his pupils to:

Advance the inside hip to initiate the turn, allowing the outside shoulder to go back no more than the small amount that the hip had rotated forwards.

- The inside hand, raised slightly, 'invites' the horse to turn, flexing his head to the inside, the fingers squeezing the rein as if squeezing water out of a sponge (or, with an advanced horse, merely vibrating the rein), so that the rider sees no more than the horse's inside eye and nostril.
- The outside hand, lowered, is held against the horse's neck so that the rein touches all along it, acting as a barrier to prevent the outward drift through the shoulder.
- The inside leg, acting 'at the girth' (the toe, not the whole foot, should be in line with the girth), encourages the inside hindleg to step under, while the outside leg, positioned about one hand's width behind the girth, controls the quarters, preventing any outward swing.

THE EFFECT OF THE WEIGHT AID

When the weight aid *is* actually taught, it is more common for the instructor to teach the student to turn the shoulders to the inside and put more weight on the inside stirrup. This does act to transfer more weight to the inside and generally has the desired effect, but I have found that it often causes the pupil to collapse her outside hip. The inside seatbone tends to slide sideways across the saddle, so that the rider is actually sitting crookedly, the one situation we should be trying to avoid at all costs! This method also encourages the rider's outside hip to move forward, with the result that the outside leg will again be used from the knee, with the heel drawn up.

The world's greatest riders and teachers have all taught the turning of the shoulders to the inside, but I have watched many of them for hours and seldom have I seen any of them actually doing it themselves! Only last night, I watched six hours of rare video footage of the late Portuguese maestro Nuno Oliveira, arguably the greatest Classical horseman of the century (and to my mind, unquestionably so). Nuno insisted on his pupils turning the shoulders to the inside, and yet watching him ride at least half a dozen horses I noticed that at all times his shoulders hardly moved, and certainly never noticeably to the inside, except in shoulder-in (we will be looking at shoulder-in in depth in Chapter 11, when the necessity not to turn the shoulders to the inside in

At my yard, we have one particularly wonderful schoolmaster, owned and bred by Margaret Cox. Margh Andante – Dandy to his friends – an 18-year-old Trakehner/Thoroughbred cross, has been blessed with the benefit of correct, Classical training throughout his life. Riders often expect Warmbloods to be a little less sharp and heavier to ride than pure Thoroughbreds, but when riding Dandy for the first time they are in for a surprise! Not only is he very light to ride, he is also extremely weight sensitive. He takes enormous delight in doing things wrong, when the student is sure that she is right! Any excessive movement or inadvertent shift of weight in the saddle, however small, will have Dandy – wearing a malevolent grin – wiggling like a worm all over the school.

The more he wiggles, the more the student tries to over-correct him, resulting in the complete opposite of what she is expecting! When negotiating a corner in the school, most riders will turn their shoulders to the inside and pull back, even if only slightly, on the inside rein. In response, Dandy drifts outwards into the corner – which, after all, is where the rider's weight is telling him to go. He then stops, facing the next wall, turns his head round and looks at me, as if to say, 'Well, are you going to come and get me out of here?' He will not move until I go over and direct the rider correctly. When turning across the school, if the student moves her shoulders to the inside and brings the inside hand back even a fraction, Dandy performs a rather mangled shoulder-in along the wall (for reasons which will become clear in Chapter 11), to the total frustration of his rider. Some riders have been so indoctrinated to turn their shoulders excessively to the inside that it has taken several lessons on Dandy before they have managed even a single turn off the track and change of rein across the diagonal!

However, the instant that the rider gets the weight right, the old horse turns with the utmost ease, and you can almost hear him sigh, 'Oh, shucks, I suppose I've had my fun, I had better do it properly now!' A horse such as this is of inestimable value as a teacher. After all, there is no point in having a schoolmaster that deludes the student by doing things right when the rider is getting it wrong.

Riding Dandy without a bridle, so proving to my students how easily he will turn and execute movements when the rider gets the weight aids right, *not* by pulling on the reins

normal turns and circles will, I hope, become abundantly clear!). It is very important not to move the shoulders consciously either forward or back, but to allow them merely to mirror the angle of the hips, just as we would naturally do when turning on foot. When walking, we do not try to contort our bodies by turning our shoulders one way and our hips the other, so why should we turn ourselves into human corkscrews when mounted on a horse?

RIDING CIRCLES

Circles are perhaps one of the hardest exercises for the novice rider to perform correctly. When I was learning, any deviation from perfect roundness would earn the rebuke from Desi Lorent, in his strong Franco-Belgian accent, 'Zat was not a circle, zat was a squashed tomato!' We were made to ride circles again and again, until they were perfectly round. Margaret Cox, my next trainer, once actually had the comment 'Circles too round' on a dressage test sheet – it seems that particular judge had seen so many 'squares with the corners knocked off' that when presented with a true circle, it appeared 'too round'!

I have always found it useful to mark four tangent points to the circle to be ridden and to think of riding four quarter circles. Particularly when riding in a fenced school, you will most likely find that the horse tends to try to drift (again through the outside shoulder) on the quarter circle that leads back to the track. In order to correct this tendency, think of first riding the four tangent points in straight lines to form a diamond shape. It is then very easy to make a slight curve, and the circle has almost drawn itself. Obviously, for young and unschooled horses, the larger the circle, the easier it is for them to perform. As the horse becomes more supple, the circle can be made smaller.

With young horses, I do not like to bore them by endlessly riding circles. I prefer to execute numerous turns, shallow loops, serpentines, and so on, in walk, all the time ensuring that the horse is bent around my inside leg. In this way, the horse quickly becomes handy and manoeuvrable, and is soon able to perform full circles without difficulty.

PRACTISING THE AIDS

For the rider's benefit, it really helps to try riding the diamonds, then ultimately the circles, on a loose rein, using the inside hip and outside leg to guide the horse. This will help to familiarize you with the co-ordination of the aids, the weight and seat being predominant in any case – so many riders think 'hands first', when they should be the *least* predominant of the aids. In time, as the horse becomes accustomed to increasingly refined aids, the smallest shift in weight or merest vibration of the rein will be sufficient to indicate to him what is required. So often I see riders, even Grand Prix level, still 'shouting' their aids at the horse, using signals which are more obvious than those which would be necessary to teach a young, green horse. As soon as the horse understands, try experimenting with minimizing the aids, however gradually. The whole concept of Classical riding is for horse and rider to move as one, with the aids being so discreet that the rider appears to be doing absolutely nothing.

PRACTICAL BENEFITS

It is beneficial for both horse and rider to practise all sorts of exercises that incorporate turns and circles. Exercises such as the demi-volte – where the horse makes a change of rein through a half circle back to the track – shallow loops, serpentines and squares can all be used to increase the horse's suppleness and the rider's dexterity. These exercises can be performed one after the other, so that the horse is making frequent changes of bend and direction, which not only helps to supple him, but also keeps his attention. Very often, riders just work on the track, or on a 20m circle, until the horse is bored silly and starts to turn his attention to other more interesting pursuits – such as shying at his own shadow, or any available object that may be in or around the school!

Making the horse more supple renders him more manoeuvrable, and therefore safer to ride in tricky situations. He can turn more quickly, and within his own length – anyone who has towed a trailer with a long-wheelbased vehicle, as opposed to a short-wheelbased one, will immediately understand what I mean! When the horse is stiff and unable to bend, he will take more time and more space to turn. If avoiding action is needed when, for instance, you are out on the roads, the quicker a horse responds to an aid which will move him out of the way, the sooner he, and you, will be out of danger. Many of the movements that we teach the dressage horse have practical applications on an everyday basis, and we will be examining these in Chapter 11.

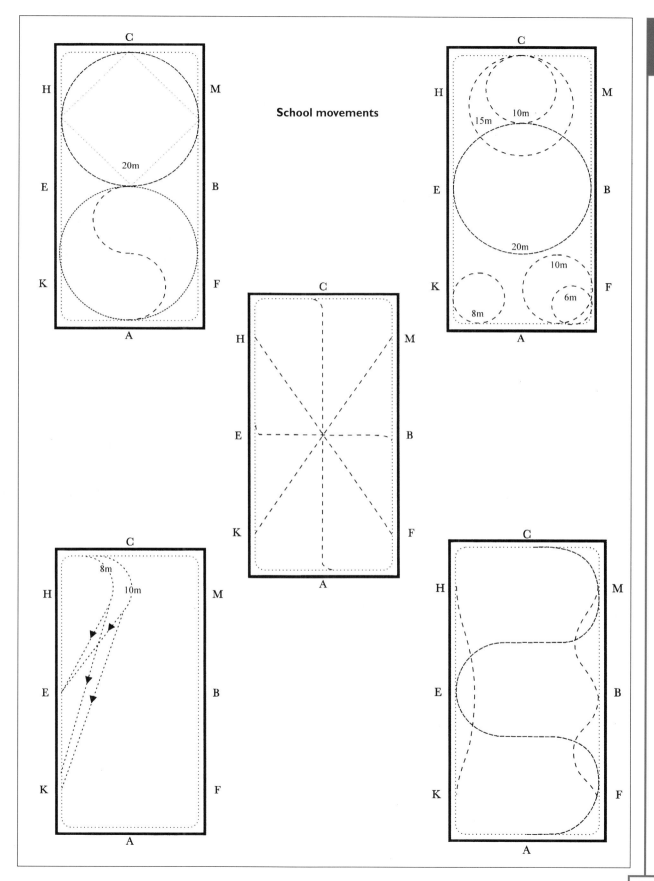

School movements

9 TRANSITIONS AND THE HALF-HALT

In simple terms, a 'transition' is a change from one pace to another, or a change in the length of stride within a pace. So, walk to trot, trot to canter, trot to walk and so on are transitions between the paces, while collected canter to medium canter and back to collected canter, for example, would constitute transitions with the pace.

GOOD TRANSITIONS

Good transitions are of paramount importance in schooling and, correctly carried out, can transform the way of going of even rather mediocre horses. So often in dressage tests one sees rough, obvious transitions, with consequent loss of marks. Most riders will have experienced the difficulty of learning to master transitions, but judging by the number that still need help when they attend my courses and clinics, often after many years of riding experience, it is an area that needs careful, step-by-step clarification.

The rider will be capable of executing good transitions only when she is able to co-ordinate her aids easily, applying them in just the right amount and at exactly the right time. Again, only practice makes perfect, and preferably on plenty of different horses. For the one- or two-horse owner this is impractical, so it helps to get together with friends and ride each other's horses, in order to gain a greater insight into the feel, which is different for each and every horse. The basic aids are the same, but each horse will require a little more or a little less of a particular aid, applied at a different split second!

We looked at the explanation and application of the aids in Chapters 5 and 6. Now we need to put them to practical use to achieve smooth transitions, which will increase the engagement and activity of the horse's hindquarters, and enable progress to be made in all other areas of schooling. Even at the highest levels of dressage, there are some riders who are more masterly

Watching dressage riders warming up at Aachen International Show in Germany a couple of years ago, I was particularly impressed by the way Klaus Balkenhol rode his transitions. Everything appeared seamless, flowing from one pace to another, or from collected to extended gaits, with no 'joins' visible. It was a tribute to – and the hallmark of – his correct Classical training methods, that each of the three horses he rode in the competitions there went in exactly the same way.

in their grasp and use of transitions than others.

A good transition should give the rider the feeling of the horse's back lifting under her seat, with a real sense of a smooth surge of power, which is not abrupt or violent in any way. I tried to explain the feeling to a friend who had ridden for years out hacking but had recently taken up dressage. We were out in his very powerful speedboat one day, and as we skimmed along he pulled down the throttle, the bow rose out of the water as the stern pushed down into it, and we zoomed off smoothly at exhilarating speed. 'Now *that's* what a good transition should feel like!' I explained – a feeling of the hindquarters lowering and the shoulders raising, with an effortless flow of power.

PREREQUISITES

When schooling horses, it is essential that the rider understands exactly what she is asking, because if the rider doesn't understand, how can the horse be expected to? In all transitions, whether upward or downward, the horse must respond immediately to the aids, remaining in the correct outline and stepping through from behind. Most riders will have noticed that if the horse is going to lose his outline it is invariably during a transition, and will have found that even going from halt to walk the horse tries to poke his nose and drop his back! With a young or unschooled horse, whose topline is undeveloped, this is because he finds it easier to raise his head and hollow his back than to raise his back and lower his head. However, the former will actually put *more* strain on the horse, and if allowed to continue indefinitely will start to produce back problems and their attendant evasions.

The horse's back is much stronger when it is raised like a bridge than when it is slung low like a hammock. In schooling the horse we are strengthening that bridge, and in most cases prolonging his working life by fittening him for the purpose of riding. Riding transitions correctly greatly enhances the horse's ability to lower his hindquarters and raise his back, but in order to achieve smooth, seamless transitions, the horse must be free from all resistance. The most important prerequisite for a good transition is the relaxation of the horse's jaw, which we examined in Chapter 6. With tension here, the horse will never work throughout his body without resistance. If he

Resisting with the jaw set (above); the jaw relaxed (below)

sets his jaw against your hand, the only way to keep him in an outline is through force, physically holding his head in place, which many riders (particularly ladies) do not have the strength to do. Sadly, many dressage trainers these days believe that it is necessary to have many kilos of weight in the hands. God help us, if to school horses we all need to develop biceps that would go ten rounds with a heavyweight boxing champion!

We now need to talk through the whole process of making transitions step by step, in order to reach a true understanding of what we as riders are asking the horse to do. So many riders find transitions really difficult, but approached logically, the process is simple.

UPWARD TRANSITIONS

Starting at the halt, and using your fingers as described on pages 44–5, ask the horse to relax his lower jaw. The instant that he does this, which will result in him lowering his head of his own accord, reward him by opening your fingers. Do this a few times before you consider moving off in walk.

Max is hollowing and coming against the hand in transition

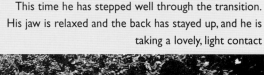

This time he has stepped well through the transition. His jaw is relaxed and the back has stayed up, and he is taking a lovely, light contact

WALK

When you do close your legs and ask for the transition into walk, you will probably find that the horse does try to raise his head and poke his nose. This is quite a normal reaction for the horse, who at this early stage in his training finds it much less effort to drop his back and trail his hindlegs out behind him than to step under with his hindlegs, raising and bridging the back, with his head remaining in the correct position.

Be ready for him. Bring him back to a halt and ask again with the fingers, until he relaxes his jaw and lowers his head. At that moment, close your lower leg to ask for forward movement, but continue to 'ask' with your fingers as he steps forwards so that his jaw will remain soft, his back will stay up and he will push through the transition by stepping well under with his hindlegs, rather than pulling himself along with his forelegs and leaving the hindlegs trailing out behind.

TROT

This procedure is basically the same as for the transition into trot, when once again the horse will often try to raise his head and avoid stepping through from behind. As the horse becomes stronger through schooling, it will become almost second nature for him to remain in the correct outline throughout all transitions, with the rider doing nothing more with the hand than giving a small vibration of the fingers to maintain relaxation of the lower jaw.

CANTER

Canter transitions are possibly the most difficult to achieve smoothly in the early stages, and require very careful timing of the aid. With young horses, I tend not to work too much on the canter in the school for quite some time, unless they show a particular aptitude and balance. It is far better just to canter in straight lines out hacking to start with, so that the horse finds his own balance and does not worry about actually getting into canter. As my indoor school here is only 15m wide, I rarely ask horses to canter until they are working in reasonable early collection in trot. Through numerous walk to trot transitions in succession, the horse builds up impulsion, until one day he will offer canter, often even from walk. In this way, the canter starts round and balanced, not flat and elongated, as is often the case when the horse is allowed to run faster and faster in trot, until he has no option but to fall into canter.

The aids

The aids for canter have to be timed just right in order for the horse to strike off with the correct lead. The rider's slightly raised inside hand, fingers squeezing or vibrating the rein, flexes the horse's head to the inside, just enough to see the inside eye and nostril, with the outside rein lowered in support at the base of the neck. The rider's outside leg instigates the first beat of canter, and the inside leg simultaneously applies pressure at the girth to push the horse's inside leg underneath the body, in turn lifting and lightening the shoulders to give lightness and expression to the canter. The inside leg is the predominant one of the two, acting at the girth in a very slight inward and forwards 'nudge', as if brushing the coat in the wrong direction, mentally giving the rider the feeling of 'scooping' the horse's inside hindleg up and under him.

Improving the canter

Frequent transitions are the secret of improving the quality of the pace. I often see instructors making their pupils canter on long after the quality of the pace has been lost, in the mistaken belief that they can push the horse out of it. This is not the case. When they are learning, riders can only hold their position and balance for a few strides at a time before losing it. I insist on them doing frequent transitions, gradually increasing

Here Juniper has caught Donna out in the transition and has raised her head. Quality of the canter will be more difficult to establish and maintain

In this transition, Donna has maintained a round outline, with head lower, and Juniper will be able to 'jump' through her canter strides, not flatten; contact would be lightened by opening the fingers within the next two strides

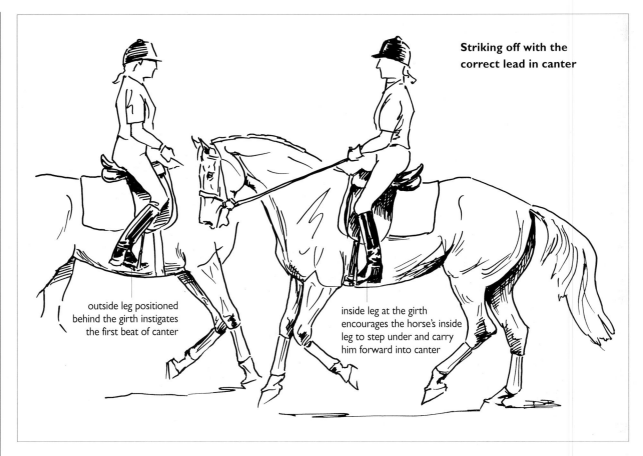

Striking off with the correct lead in canter

outside leg positioned behind the girth instigates the first beat of canter

inside leg at the girth encourages the horse's inside leg to step under and carry him forward into canter

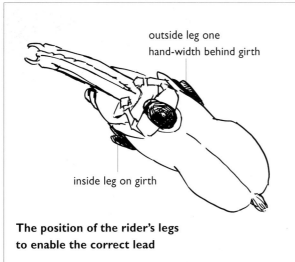

outside leg one hand-width behind girth

inside leg on girth

The position of the rider's legs to enable the correct lead

and remains 'uphill' throughout. Gradually, as the horse's confidence and strength increase, the number of canter strides can also be increased, until he can manage a complete 20m circle without dropping on to his shoulders. Every stride in canter should feel like a little jump, an uphill bound, giving life and expression to the movement. This 'uphill' quality will be especially needed later to perform canter pirouettes and flying changes in sequence.

Walk to canter

There still seems to be an attitude (at least in the UK) that walk to canter is quite an advanced movement. Provided that they are working in a correct outline and are reasonably well engaged behind, most horses actually find it easier than trot to canter, when it is all too easy for the horse to run and lose balance. It is also much easier for novice riders to achieve, when riding a schoolmaster who will effortlessly pop up into canter from walk with a simple aid, instead of running faster and faster in trot until he has no option but to canter. By this time the rider is usually wishing that she hadn't eaten prior to the lesson, as she is thoroughly jolted

the number of strides as their balance and muscle tone improve, and this is exactly the same for the horse.

By doing no more than perhaps eight to ten strides of canter before returning to trot, re-establishing the balance, and then moving up into canter again for a similar number of strides, the rider ensures that the horse does not fall on to his forehand

Frequent canter transitions maintain and enhance the uphill quality of the canter – here the pony has come just a little against the hand and needs to relax his jaw a little more

about in the saddle! The horse, needless to say, also stiffens his back against the rider's bouncing around, making the canter harder than ever to absorb.

TRANSITIONS WITHIN THE PACE

I do not ask the horse to lengthen his stride until he is confirmed in his ability to show some collection. I do wish that dressage tests in the UK would not ask for horses to show a lengthening of stride so early on in the grades. It encourages horses to run and to flatten rather than raise the back, flicking the toe out from the knee instead of moving from the shoulder. Riders often tell me that they find extended paces very difficult to sit to. They shouldn't! If the horse is working correctly, raising his back and lifting his

shoulders, the movement will feel big but not in the least uncomfortable. It should give the rider the impression of being carried along on the crest of a wave, the back rippling under her, not shooting her skywards as will happen if the back is stiff and the horse is flat and running. To obtain lengthened strides, close the legs to encourage the hindlegs to step further under. At the same time, open the fingers a little to allow the horse to lengthen his neck.

If you obtain only two or three lengthened steps at first, be satisfied. Ask for more, and the horse will flatten. As he strengthens, ask for a few more lengthened strides, always returning to collected trot as soon as you feel him lose the lift. Before long, you will be able to ask for a little more, to produce medium trot. Again, the horse will most likely be able

A couple of years ago, I held a lecture demonstration at a large equestrian college. I intended to take one horse, but also wanted to use two of the college's working pupils with ordinary school horses on which to assess them, plus a lunge horse which would go easily from walk to canter. The stable manager seemed at a loss to know why I wanted a horse that would do this. A few days later she rang back, informing me that she had procured two working pupil 'guinea pigs' for me, with two school horses as I had requested. She then went on to say that she had also found me a lunge horse that would indeed perform walk to canter, and had obtained the services of a 'good' rider to put on the horse, on the lunge.

When I explained that I wanted the lunge horse to put the working pupils on, after first seeing them ride the school horses to assess their problems, the stable manager nearly had apoplexy! 'You can't put working pupils on a horse that does walk to canter!' she exclaimed. I calmly asked her, since when had walk to canter been considered a Grand Prix movement, and explained that any horse should be capable of performing it with a modicum of schooling. Her tone implied the contempt she obviously considered I deserved!

to manage only a few strides without flattening. Build up gradually, as before. This is equally applicable to extended trot, and the same rules apply to achieving medium and extended canter.

If the horse is schooled in this way, always ensuring that the transitions are as smooth as possible, the work will remain fluent and effortless. By ensuring that the horse does not become tired and sore by overdoing the teaching of any movement, resistance and evasion can be avoided almost entirely. Always bear in mind that the quality of the gait is far more important than the quantity. *Quantity* will only be possible where *quality* is present.

DOWNWARD TRANSITIONS

Most riders find downward transitions even more difficult to ride smoothly than upward ones. This is invariably because the rider attempts to use too much hand to slow down, so that the horse pulls back against the rein, resulting in a rough and uneven change of pace. The horse is also likely to try to raise his head in defence against a strong use of the rein, dropping his back in consequence, so that he does not step 'through' the transition from behind. The predominant aid used in downward transitions must always be the seat (see page 48),

Transitions within the pace: moving from collected to extended trot

otherwise the horse will come up against the hand, shorten and compress the neck, and drop his weight on to his shoulders, instead of bringing it back on to his quarters.

THE AIDS

All downward transitions are effectively the same, whether they be from walk to halt, trot to walk, canter to trot or any other combination. In order to make a downward transition, simultaneously close your lower leg, to keep the horse's hindlegs travelling under rather than trailing behind, and your seat/upper thigh muscles. The horse feels the difference between you moving with him, and you then arresting that movement by tightening your buttock muscles and upper thighs. It is not an action that causes the horse discomfort, because it lightens your seat in the saddle, enabling him to lift and round his back with ease. As in upward transitions, there is a danger of the horse attempting to raise his head and drop his back; to prevent this, maintain the relaxation of his lower jaw by the use of your fingers. It may take a little stronger finger tension on the reins – this should never be in a backward-pulling manner but, as always, by closing the fingers

Downward transition – horse coming against the hand which rider is using too strongly instead of her seat – hindlegs not stepping through

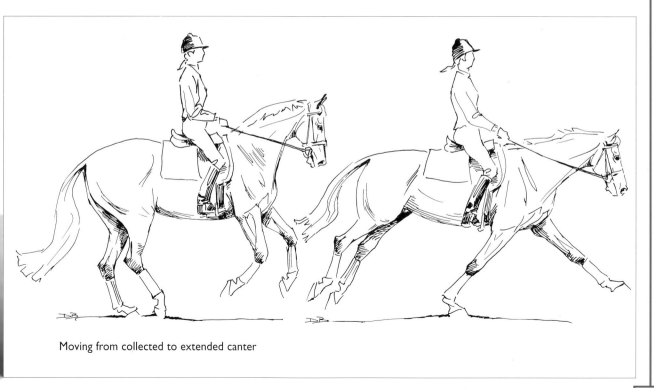

Moving from collected to extended canter

of alternate hands as if squeezing water out of a sponge. The instant that the horse responds, by softening in your hand, reward him by opening your fingers and releasing the tension.

Gradually, you will learn to feel how much or how little tension each horse requires. The more conversant the horse becomes with the aid, through progressive schooling, the lighter the aid needed to achieve the result. The timing is also crucial, particularly at the beginning of schooling, because the horse will often be quick to snatch up his head when you least expect it. Be vigilant, and learn to feel the split second that the jaw tightens, reacting instantly to vibrate or squeeze your fingers on the reins to restore the relaxation. Each horse will require slightly more or less of any aid, according to his sensitivity and way of going. Students cannot believe how incredibly light my own Arabian stallion is to ride – you have to do almost nothing, to achieve everything!

With each and every horse that you ride, experiment with the aids to see how much or little you need. Always start off with a light aid and increase in strength, rather than the other way round; otherwise, if the horse turns out to be super-sensitive, you may get rather more reaction than you require!

RISING TROT

Downward transitions in rising trot need a different approach, but the principle is still the same – that is, minimal use of the hand. The usual method taught to make downward transitions in rising trot is to go

Watch the average rising trot to walk transition. The rider goes along in rising trot, decides to make a transition, sits down with a thud in the saddle, having had to alter her upper body alignment from just in front of the vertical to vertical, often with a consequent loss of balance, and pulls back on the reins in the process. The horse, objecting to the thud in the saddle, drops his back and pokes his nose in the air, often slowing almost to the point of halting. The rider panics, and closes both legs or gives him a kick, whereupon the horse breaks back into trot! The whole process then has to be repeated. I have seen this happen more times than I could count, and yet, even with novice pupils, it can be avoided.

through a few strides of sitting trot before returning to walk. Time and again, I have seen instructors trying to improve their pupils' downward transitions in rising trot, practising them over and over, but never seeming to get much better. I know, because I used to be one of them! After Margaret Cox taught me a different way, I began to wonder how I had been so blind for so long.

Simply by slowing your rise – deliberately coming very slightly behind the movement – and momentarily closing your seat and thigh muscles as your seat returns to the saddle, the horse will quickly respond and drop back to walk. Initially, it may take perhaps six strides to achieve this, so the transition is progressive, but within a couple of schooling sessions, the horse will realize what you want and will return to walk smoothly and easily within only two strides, as he feels you slow your body weight and fall just a fraction out of sync with his stride. Instead of his back dropping and his head raising, as with the transition through sitting trot, his head will stay down and his back will remain up. To ensure that the horse steps through the transition without faltering and losing rhythm, at the first step of walk use your legs as described on page 39, in time with the swing of his belly – left, right, left, right – encouraging each hindleg in turn as it leaves the ground to step well under the body. In this way, you will achieve a smooth, instant downward transition, with no loss of rhythm or impulsion.

PRACTICAL BENEFITS

Transitions improve rider control. There is nothing better for a novice rider than to practise frequent changes of pace. In this way, the horse doesn't have as much chance to gather the momentum that would enable him to cart his rider who, through transitions, will bring the horse into a rounder outline and thus much more under control. Transitions can also be carried out when hacking along quiet lanes or bridleways. Use a tree, telegraph pole or other fixed point as a marker, and aim to make your transition at that spot. Your horse will probably be a little mystified to begin with, particularly if he is used to walking or trotting for some distance without changing gait, but persevere. You will ultimately gain more control, and the horse will maintain better concentration. There is no rule which says that schooling can only take place in a school!

IMPROVING THE 'LAZY' HORSE

Transitions will also help to make a lazy horse more active, by storing up a little energy with each correct change of pace. When a horse is lazy and won't go forward from the leg, I normally give a sharp tap with a dressage whip just behind my leg at the same moment that I apply the leg aid. Generally this is sufficient to waken the horse into activity. I do not believe in using spurs on lazy horses, because they often resent them and will back off all the more. Some idle horses also resent the use of the whip, and will buck and even squeal if the whip is used at all. I find that such horses respond far better to a lunge whip. Used behind them, with a bit of a crack, the noise is usually sufficient to startle them into moving forwards and swishing the lash around their hocks is then enough to maintain forward movement. I am not entirely sure why this works with so many lazy equines. It obviously has something to do with the fact that it is coming from behind, where they (a) can't see it coming, (b) don't expect it and (c) don't connect it with the rider.

I frequently find that lazy horses have not been born that way. Either they have been very badly ridden from an early age and have had their sides kicked to oblivion, and/or they have never been taught *what the leg actually means*. When the horse makes the connection between the cracking or swishing of the lunge whip and the closing of the rider's leg, it is not long before the penny drops and he begins to respond to correct leg aids.

THE HALF-HALT

There is a lot of mystique attached to the half-halt. What exactly is it? There are, I suppose, two schools of thought on the subject.

1 You will often hear instructors say, 'Half-halt with the outside rein', which generally means give a little check with the rein before attempting to perform a movement, rather like a driving instructor telling his pupil to check in the rearview mirror before making any manoeuvre.

2 The other school maintains that it is a complete rebalancing effect, in that when correctly performed it shifts the weight to the rear of the horse, lightening the forehand and freeing the shoulders.

I tend to subscribe to the latter thinking. A true half-halt should be ju t that – a slowing of the pace until the horse almost drops back to the pace below,

but is immediately asked to go forward again. This has the effect of transferring the weight backwards, thereby further engaging the hind end. The second in Kalman de Jurenak's wonderful series of *Classical Schooling* videos shows some superb examples of correct half-halts. One of my pupils remarked very aptly that these were like a 'freeze frame' effect.

The half-halt where the rider merely checks with the outside rein is what the French Classical School termed an *arrête*, a little 'stop' with the hand – a warning of a movement about to be requested. A true half-halt is used throughout schooling at frequent intervals, to re-engage the hocks and lighten the forehand. It cannot, however, be performed until the horse is easily able to carry out correct full transitions, both upward and downward, immediately on request.

THE AIDS

The half-halt is asked for using the same aids as for a downward transition, but releasing them a fraction before the horse drops down to the pace below and then asking him to go forwards again immediately. The easiest way to teach the horse the half-halt is gradually to reduce the number of strides between full transitions. For example, start with trot, six strides of walk, trot. Reduce the number of walk strides gradually, until the horse can easily do trot, one stride of walk, trot. As soon as he can cope with this, ask for the half-halt, as described above. Once the horse is familiar with the half-halt, use it at any time, many times, in a schooling session, if the pace has become a little tired and needs a quick boost to get the horse back on his hocks. 'Refresh the movement', as Dr Reiner Klimke puts it.

IMPROVING 'FEEL'

Transitions and half-halts, then, are two of the greatest 'tools' that we have to improve the horse's way of going. Learning to execute really smooth and accurate transitions is the next stage on in rider 'feel' (see Chapter 4). Once you have acquired this ability, you will find that schooling horses really does become much easier.

From there on, your 'feel' will increase daily, until you are so in tune with your horse that you will be able to make minute readjustments to his balance and impulsion almost unconsciously, without needing to think about it. At this stage, you can begin to call yourself a rider, and not merely a passenger!

GIBSON

Champion Connemara mare, Shipton Sea Image

Canter is always thought of as one of the more difficult paces to improve. When looking for a dressage or showjumping horse, an 'uphill' canter is a great asset. Although it is indeed harder to improve something that is not naturally present, it is possible. I have worked with many horses and ponies that do not have a naturally good, round, uphill balance in canter. In particular, two Connemara ponies that I train come to mind.

The first is a mare, Shipton Sea Image, 14 years old when we began schooling, who had won just about everything it is possible to win for her breed but was stuck firmly at Novice level in dressage. I had noticed her around the shows over several years and had often thought that I would love to work with her, as I could

see that she had much more to give than she was able to offer at that time. Image's rider, Debbie Mumford, is a talented all-round horsewoman, who wished to increase her dressage knowledge, and to further the pony's career, which at that point seemed to be at a stalemate, so she asked me, to my delight, to help. Image is a very spooky pony, given to seeing gremlins in every corner of a dressage arena, or even in the school at home. I repainted the indoor school kicking boards white, and she refused to go near them for the next three weeks! Image was regularly marked down in tests for going crookedly, hadn't the best walk, and a rather short, earthbound canter. Her trot, whilst rhythmic, was not as expressive as it could be. Work on plenty of transitions to get her 'in front of the leg' had her moving very differently, even on her first lesson.

Much work too on basic lateral exercises, shoulder-

in, and travers in particular, at walk, soon straightened her, and she has never been marked down for crookedness since. The lateral work in walk also helped to improve the pace, the walk being much less hurried and more even. Frequent transitions from walk to trot, and trot to walk, then halt-trot, trot-halt gave the pace much more lift and expression, so much so that Image began to be mistaken for a little Lipizzaner! We began to work on the lateral work in trot, and we also began to develop the medium trot.

Within six weeks of beginning the work with her, I had been asked at one day's notice to fill in for another dressage trainer at a lecture demonstration near Bristol, so whisked Debbie and Image off to act as demonstration models. The usually spooky mare had plenty to look at – flower tubs, white boards and all – but behaved really well; she had no intention of making a fool of herself in front of 300 people! Many

of them came up to me afterwards to say that they were amazed by her medium trot that looked nearly airborne (the extended trot that was to come later was even more spectacular), and by her ability to cross and sweep sideways in the lateral movements.

Giving Image so much more to learn seemed to take the edge off her 'spookiness' and she became much more settled, beating good Warmbloods and achieving scores of over 70 per cent, with her previously typical mark of between 4 and 6 for walk and canter, going up to 7s for the walk, and even 9s for the canter Debbie is a very easy rider to teach, having particularly good timing and feel, which greatly contributed to Image's rapid progress, competing to medium level within a year. Her owner, Marion Ash, of Beenleighford Stud, then decided to retire her as a broodmare, as the stud had younger ponies coming on that required Debbie's time.

Image's half-brother is a very different type of pony. Also a purebred Connemara, by the same sire, he is quite different in type. Originally also ridden by Debbie Mumford, he had been sold the previous year, but the new owners now wanted her to have him back to school him and show him in native pony classes for them. Debbie has since bought him back!

Rarely have I seen such a dreadful walk – he was like an old gent in carpet slippers! Shuffling along, he certainly did not have four clear beats – he didn't even go in two-time, as some horses are prone to doing. Everything seemed very random and irregular: he appeared merely to put his feet down when and where the moment dictated! On the other hand, the pony's trot proved to be rather good, rhythmic and with natural spring, but the canter was as disastrous as the walk. Ker plonk, ker plonk, it resounded, as he dropped heavily on to his forehand at every stride. I decided that

I would work on the walk, and develop the trot, but ignore the canter until later.

I improved the walk by literally teaching the pony to place one foot after the other. This was achieved by slowing the walk right down through holding with my seat, then releasing at the right moment and using my leg on that side to send the hindleg under, then allowing the foreleg to go forward, holding momentarily with my seat again, using my other leg to engage the opposite hind, then releasing my seat again to allow the other foreleg forward, and so on. Within a few sessions, we had a four-time walk. Admittedly, it will never be a worldbeater, but at least it is a walk!

Working the pony through many transitions in trot to improve his natural spring and elasticity, it was not unexpected that one day, having built up the impulsion into early collection, he sprang from walk to canter instead of walk to trot. I can honestly say that even I did not expect what followed. Every stride was a copybook uphill jump, performed with utmost ease, even round a full 20m circle. Neither was this just a one-off fluke: his canter is now, without question, his best pace. It is still not natural to him, though, as when turned out in the field I am always amused to see (and hear!) him dropping down on his shoulders in his earlier customary fashion when under saddle. Like his half-sister, this pony has proved to have great aptitude for lateral work, and within a few months of starting work with him, he won a reserve national breed title.

Beenleighford Moonraker (Moon) –
champion Connemara

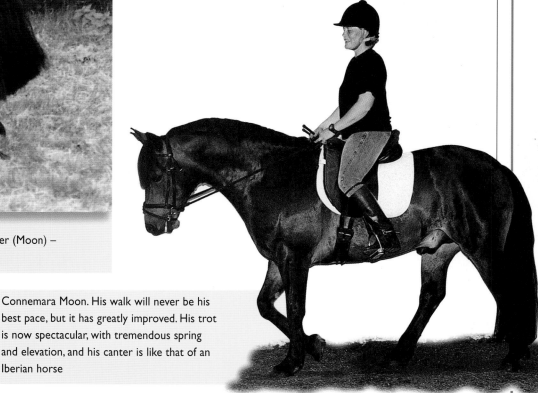

Connemara Moon. His walk will never be his best pace, but it has greatly improved. His trot is now spectacular, with tremendous spring and elevation, and his canter is like that of an Iberian horse

Some time ago, I was asked to help a lady, herself a retired instructor in her sixties, with her gelding, who had something of a reputation for being an ungenerous, lazy, 'couch potato' of a horse, who never offered anything willingly. He was actually a rather nice-looking horse, well made and with quality, so he really appeared to have little excuse for his behaviour.

His owner arrived for her lesson armed with two dressage whips, one for either hand, and a pair of fairly formidable spurs. As soon as she tried to use any weapon from her armoury, the horse bucked, squealed and dug his toes in ever more firmly. I asked to ride him, as he seemed very resistant in his lower jaw. Sure enough, he was like riding a tank, leaning on the hand almost constantly. I asked to borrow a pelham bit from the stable manager, and then rode the horse in it for a few more minutes. By this time, a small assembly had gathered in the indoor school gallery, as the horse had quite a reputation in the area! The horse willingly softened and relaxed his jaw within a minute of changing to the pelham, lowering his head as I had hoped and expected. However, it still had not occurred to him that I also required him to move forward!

I put his owner back up again, and asked her to play gently with her fingers on the reins, to obtain the same relaxation that he had willingly given me. This achieved, I then cracked the lunge whip behind him at the same time as his rider closed her legs around his sides. He shot forward, startled, before settling back to his usual shuffle. We repeated the

Top: Here Max is resisting because Jo is pulling back, not 'asking' with the fingers
Left: Again, in canter, Max is 'against the hand'

exercise several times more, this time with me swishing the whip around his hocks after first cracking it behind him. We had already dispensed with the armoury, and within a few minutes I had to ask his rider to slow down the tempo, as the horse's enthusiasm was beginning to get the better of him. It was almost as if he was saying, 'Whoopee, look at me, I can move!'

My aim was to work the horse in the long and low position, so that he learned to stretch over his back while still stepping well under with his hocks, taking half the number of steps but covering twice the distance at each stride. This we achieved in a few more minutes, and the audience began to look at this horse in a new light. Gone was the heavy-footed thump, thump, at the trot – instead, he sprang lightly from diagonal pair to diagonal pair with his back swinging, and remained softly on the bit. Working him then through many transitions, he even began to offer a few steps of passage. He looked so incredibly proud and pleased with himself that it was quite touching to witness. Gone was the sour-faced, ears-flat and tail-clamped horse of less than an hour earlier, a horse to which you would hardly have given a second glance. By showing him that he could do it, and how, we had given him back his pride.

It took several more sessions to consolidate the improvement, with a friend working him from the ground with the lunge whip, but he has never looked back since. His owner is delighted with her forward-going horse, and is well on her way to forging a real partnership with him.

Above: I'm asking Max to relax his jaw, by squeezing with the fingers of alternate hands – *never* with backward traction!

Here, Max is starting to yield his jaw, and doesn't look nearly so cross!

Max is now accepting the bit; he is not short in the neck, the contact is light, and his expression relaxed and happy

Owner Jo is back aboard. Max has dropped the contact here and come behind the bit because she is using her hand too strongly. Jo's lower leg is too far back and she has not been able to push him up from behind

Max is back 'on the bit' and looking much less tense in the neck and jaw because Jo has released the tension

In this shot, taken a few minutes later, Jo has achieved a lovely outline with Max – soft, round, light. He is not yet quite tracking up, but is working within his own tempo, which will develop the spring to enhance the pushing power, from whence comes the impulsion

Corpus, 9-year-old ex-racehorse – just started re-schooling as an eventer.

Here, he is resisting by raising his head and stiffening his lower jaw, and his back is like a plank to sit on! Hindlegs trailing

Corpus starting to get the idea! Here he is accepting the bit, and lengthening his neck

Here, I am playing with his paces, to get some idea of his ability. It is obvious that he has plenty

Although he has dropped the contact, his stride is beginning to develop some spring. This is only the second time I have worked with Corpus. He has an abundance of talent – three very good paces and tremendous ability to engage his hindquarters. Here he needs to step under more but that will come!

Stephanie, Corpus' owner, back on board, allowing him to walk out freely

A nice trot for an ex-racehorse on his second lesson! This, for Corpus, is a good working trot at the moment, not too fast, but sufficiently forward to track up. His head has flexed the wrong way a little; Stephanie needed to flex a little to the right to straighten him

Here, I am working Corpus from the ground, merely touching him on the hindlegs – sometimes on the cannon bone, sometimes just above the hock, to encourage him to step under and fold the hind joints, to create more spring

Corpus is developing that spring – look at his fetlocks; see how much 'give' is in the joints. This horse could be a very good dressage horse, but Stephanie still maintains she wants him to event – he jumps like a star, too!

Corpus' fifth lesson: these photographs were taken three weeks after the first shoot. Also note the improvement in his condition.

Corpus is getting fit for the autumn eventing season, and is seen here walking out with long, free strides

For the last ten days he has been ridden in a snaffle again. Note his lovely light, springy trot, with great flexion of the fetlocks

We wanted to see if he could lengthen his stride easily: this photograph clearly shows that he can. We would not start to develop medium or extended trot at this stage, as he is not yet strong enough to maintain the spring in his joints that will give the paces expression and lift; he would simply flatten and 'run'

Here Stephanie is asking for collection in trot, not by pulling in Corpus' head and booting with her leg, but by using her seat as a collecting aid in conjunction with her lower legs

Purely to see if he could do it, Stephanie asked Corpus (after only five lessons, in six weeks of training) for a few steps of piaffe, which he offered willingly – no force was used. I'm sure he could make it as a dressage horse if eventing doesn't work out!

Corpus' control is coming on in leaps and bounds – literally! he scored 8 for one canter movement in his first dressage test

See how actively he steps under with his inside hind. He is still leaning on the hand a little in canter, but frequent transitions will continue to lighten his shoulders, resulting in a lighter action

He is still behind the vertical, but I expect him to be less prone to this tendency as his hind end takes up more weight and lightens the forehand, this should only take a few weeks

10 DEVELOPING RHYTHM, TEMPO AND EXPRESSION

Some horses, much like some human beings, seem to be born with naturally good rhythm. For those less fortunately endowed by Nature, it is up to the rider to develop and improve the paces. Each horse has his own rhythm and tempo in which he feels comfortable, and it is necessary to work within that limit to increase the flexion of the joints, which in turn will amplify the spring in the stride, leading to enhanced expression. The rhythm is the regularity of the steps in any of the paces, while the tempo is the speed of the rhythm.

As I said earlier, for some reason (which escapes me) there is a current fashion in the dressage world for rushing horses around like headless chickens, in the belief that this increases impulsion – but impulsion has nothing to do with speed. There has been a lot of debate over the last few years as to what separates Classical equitation from competition dressage, or whether indeed there is any difference at all. Sadly, there is no doubt in my own mind that there is a very real chasm between the two. Competition dressage is all about power: big-moving horses with great natural extension and flamboyance in their paces. In order to obtain maximum power, it seems to be deemed necessary to push the horse out of his own inborn rhythm – and it is then people wonder why so few horses, even at the very top levels internationally, can perform the very collected movements such as canter pirouettes and piaffe to a high standard. These movements require great collection, and if the horse has been rushing around at twice his natural tempo it is hardly surprising that he finds slowing down, while still maintaining the upward lift in the stride, very difficult.

DEVELOPING RHYTHM

Some highly-strung horses have an intrinsic tendency to rush. This is nearly always due to a lack of acceptance of the rider's leg, from which they want

Showing the difference between 'flattening' of the movement, and developing spring and expression; there is only a 10-minute gap between these two photographs – note how much happier this ex-racehorse has become in such a short time to run away rather than step under. Such horses will have a short, choppy, stilted stride and will be difficult to sustain in rhythm, until they learn to understand that the leg means 'step under', not 'run faster'. They will be uncomfortable to sit to, the equine equivalent of a pogo stick, because the back will be flat, or even hollow, and the leg joints will not be flexing but will be jarring on the ground at each stride. Most horses have been made to go in this way by poor riding. When the young horse is first backed and his education embarked upon, if he is apprehensive of the rider's leg – as some highly bred and very sensitive horses will be – he will need a similarly sensitive rider who understands his problem and can correct it at this stage, through reassurance and intuitive timing of the aids. In this way, he can be calmed, and the sensitive youngster will not develop into a hot and flighty adult.

Other, more phlegmatic types find it difficult to maintain a rhythm because they lack impulsion, and so their riders need to try to engender a bit more enthusiasm in their mount. Often, this situation arises because as a youngster the horse was not taught to go forward properly on the lunge, and then to be responsive to the leg under saddle, so he quickly settles into the habit of plodding along half-heartedly, with the rider having to push him nearly every step of the way.

In either case, the rider has to take responsibility for the rhythm.

THE RUSHING HORSE

In the first instance, the 'hot' horse that runs away from the leg must be taught that it is not something to be afraid of. To begin with, he must learn to go 'long and low', so that he stretches and lifts his back muscles and lengthens his stride. The aim should be to cover twice the ground in half the number of strides that he would take when going in his normal, hurried, tense, choppy way.

Walk

Walk the horse around on as long a rein as you dare, making frequent changes of rein and allowing him to stretch his neck and nose down, and lengthen his stride. If he wants just to poke his nose out in front, or raise his head above the point of control, do not allow this to happen. Instead, shorten your reins carefully, and then use your fingers to ask him to relax his lower jaw. As soon as you feel him soften in your hand, open your fingers and let the reins out a little, and if he offers to stretch his head and neck down, stroke his neck with one hand. If necessary, incline your upper body just a little forward, and keep your hands lowered on either side of the wither. If at first, the horse does not want to stretch, shorten the reins and repeat the exercise a few more times, until he understands that he can do so.

Trot

When the horse is quite relaxed and easy in the walk, taking long, free steps and overtracking, you can begin to think about the trot. This should always be carried out rising at this stage, particularly when riding a horse of this type. I tend to stay on the track at this stage, as the horse does not need the extra problem of balancing himself on turns and circles as well as listening to the rider. By gradually taking up the rein again, still asking the horse with your fingers to maintain the softness in his jaw, gently close your legs and ask for the transition up to rising trot. If the horse goes to 'scoot' forwards, slow your rise, close your seat and thigh muscles firmly as you sit, *keep* the leg on lightly, and at the same time squeeze the reins more strongly with the fingers of alternate hands to obtain a downward transition to walk, in as few strides as possible. Effectively, you are saying, 'No, you don't run off, my legs mean step under, not go faster.' The instant the horse has yielded and returned to walk, reward him by opening your fingers and praising him with your voice.

Repeat the exercise many times, until the horse begins to understand and offers more and more unhurried, longer steps after each transition to trot. As soon as you feel the steps start to quicken, bring him back to walk. Again, progress has to be made gradually – Rome wasn't built in a day! At this stage, introduce circles of no less 20m diameter, 15m demi-voltes and shallow loops, to increase the horse's concentration. By this time, he should be sufficiently confident to maintain a reasonable rhythm without trying to rush, except perhaps if something startles him or he momentarily loses confidence for some other reason. To bring him back into rhythm, it should be sufficient merely to slow your rise, without having to go through a downward transition to walk. In this way, the horse will learn to keep up an even tempo, his stride will lengthen and his back will start to swing. Not only will the horse feel far more comfortable to ride, his temperament will also gradually change. Keeping an even rhythm seems to have an almost soporific effect on horses – I have used these techniques to cure so many which have been deemed difficult or hot, that I could write a book of case histories on those alone!

Canter

The same rules apply in canter. If the horse tries to rush off, bring him back to trot, re-establish a calm pace, and then ask again for canter. Repeat the exercise a few times, then walk on a long rein. Do not try to do too much too soon, especially in canter – we do not want the horse to slow down purely because he is tired, but because he is becoming more confident.

Improving the canter will be even easier if the horse will go from walk to canter, as the pace will invariably start off rounder and slower. Often he will find the downward transition from canter to walk more difficult, and will want to go through a few strides of trot before returning to walk. Try to reduce the number of strides gradually, until one

day the horse will automatically go from canter straight into walk.

THE LAZY HORSE

With a horse of the opposite temperament, who is lethargic and requires a lot of rider effort to keep him moving, there is often a reason for his lack of desire to go forward. It may be that the horse has never been taught to go forward from the leg, and so doesn't understand what is required of him. Consequently, the rider kicks away at his sides to get him to move, further deadening any sensitivity to the leg in the process. See page 69 for advice on how to re-educate the lazy horse.

TURNS AND TRANSITIONS

Rhythm is also very important throughout transitions and changes of direction. You will often see a horse quicken his stride as he hurries from walk into trot, or from trot into canter. The same tends to happen when making turns, or movements including turns, when irregularities in the pace are liable to creep in. Again, it is the rider's responsibility to maintain an even rhythm throughout, by being aware of the most likely places that the horse could lose a little balance and impulsion, thereby dropping back in the rhythm. Until the horse is very well balanced and straight, do not put him into a situation where it is bound to happen by asking him to do small circles or turns, or serpentines.

If you are riding on a surface that is not absolutely even, loss of rhythm is especially liable to happen when the horse has to negotiate a patch of boggy or slippery ground. At this stage, the rider needs to help balance the horse through such situations, keeping the leg closed on – even reinforcing it with a small tap of the whip behind the leg to keep up the impulsion – and shortening the rein and closing the fingers a little, so that the horse may, for a second, prop himself up. Immediately you feel him regain his balance, open your fingers, so that he does not come to rely on the hand as a 'fifth leg' and thereby learn to lean on the bit.

When learning, during transitions the horse will take advantage of any opportunity to run into the next pace up, pulling himself along on his forehand. At this stage, he will find falling on to his forehand easier than having to propel himself forwards from behind. It can help to ride to music which is of the same beat and tempo as the horse's natural rhythm, or you can use a metronome. Try to ride the rhythm consciously throughout all transitions, so that they begin to flow smoothly from one pace into another without any visible joins.

EXPRESSION

Expression can only come about when the horse is moving with impulsion, his joints are flexing and compressing, and his whole attitude is one of *joie de vivre*. Expression cannot ever be brought about through force, and there is a huge difference in the way of going of horses that have been trained in this way and those that have been developed progressively and gymnastically in the same way as a human athlete or dancer. The latter will perform with ease and grace, bringing dressage to the status of an art form, while the former type of (so-called) 'training' will produce performances that are stilted and mechanical.

I unashamedly use videos of some of the top riders of today to illustrate to my students the difference between the two. Many are shocked when they see the graphic illustrations on the screen in front of them. I have even put total non-riders to the test, and all have quickly been able to spot the difference between those who train with force and those who use progressive Classical methods. If the difference is so obvious even to the completely untrained eye, why is it that so few horses in the competition world today are trained to work with harmony and finesse, rather than through strength and domination?

Sadly, I have personally witnessed the brutality that takes place in some of the top yards. Horses trained in this way are easily spotted by their tense,

Moon is a little straight in the hocks, but it is clear that with training his hind joints are suppling, enabling him to start to take the weight back in canter. Just how expressive his canter has now become does not seem to show in photographs; there is actually much more obvious uphill 'jump' in his canter

Moon is against the hand here, and is getting a little onward bound in medium canter

Woody, Irish Draught x TB, 7 years old, is a chunky sort of chap, not the type that most people would think to train for dressage! He is the most delightful, light, sharp, responsive ride, highly intelligent. All due credit to his owner, Debbie, who spotted his potential and has developed it

nervous faces, often accompanied by a vigorous swishing of the tail and grinding of the teeth, and a mechanical way of going. In contrast, horses that have been trained through progressive, gymnastic development, *and rewarded for their efforts*, appear proud and happy in their work. Their expression comes about through being in harmony *with* and trusting *in* their rider, whom they desire to please.

ACHIEVING TRUE EXPRESSION

So, how do we achieve this quality of expression? We have already looked at the benefits of transitions and half-halts, where the hand does not predominate and the seat is the retarding aid. Expression is developed as a by-product of good schooling where, through the retarding and collecting influence of the seat – which does not compress and shorten the horse's outline – the energy obtained is directed

upwards more than forwards, resulting in great spring and therefore lightness of footfall. The hoofbeats of a horse in high collection are not even audible, unless he is performing on a metalled surface.

True 'expression' should manifest itself in the same way as the exuberance of a horse at liberty, showing off to his friends in the field, or as stallion would prance when trying to catch the eye of a mare. When a rider can capture this very essence of the horse's spirit – through partnership, not domination – then she is a fine horsewoman indeed.

Here, Debbie has speeded up the tempo of the trot deliberately. Although Woody is stepping quite well under, he is not using his joints – the stride looks flat; he is not yet quite ready to push the stride out, yet still maintain the lift and expression

In this photo, Debbie has slowed the tempo down again, and it is obvious that Woody's joints are already flexing more, producing more upward spring. Contact could be a little lighter

In this shot, it is clear how much extra spring Woody is developing in his trot; his hindleg is really engaged. He has come a little 'deep' in front as Debbie has not been quick enough to open her fingers and 'give'. This quality of trot, with frequent transitions to lighten the shoulders, is the basis of the development of more pushing power, towards a stronger working trot without flattening and, ultimately, towards extensions

Woody's worst pace was his canter – he tended to be rather on his forehand. Lots of transitions from walk to canter and back are helping to lighten his front; his hindleg is well engaged, freeing and lifting his shoulder

Front view showing that canter is beginning to develop an 'uphill', not 'downhill', quality

Lateral work has to be one of the most useful schooling tools available to the rider.

Years ago (certainly in the UK) lateral work was considered rather advanced. I well remember being in the audience at a lecture demonstration by German-based dressage trainer, Kalman de Jurenak. He had brought with him a team of riders from the Hanoverian sales, and to our astonishment happily asked recently backed three-year-olds to do a modest degree of shoulder-in, a movement known as the shoulder-fore. At that time, if anyone in the UK had a ten-year-old horse that could perform shoulder-in, they were considered 'somebody'! During the subsequent question session, a member of the audience asked Kalman if it was normal in Germany to teach such a young horse some lateral steps. He replied that it was quite usual, because he was, after all, only asking for a small degree, not the finished article that you would see in the dressage arena. At this stage, he was using it purely as a tool to gain control of the horse's shoulders. Later, it would become a deeper lateral bend, increasing the engagement of the inside hindleg and lightening the shoulder, and would therefore also be an aid to collection.

At the same time that Jurenak's youngsters were peforming basic lateral steps, I remember being inordinately proud of my own Hanoverian x Thoroughbred schoolmaster, who could perform all lateral work and single flying changes, and taught me an enormous amount. He had the condition known as stringhalt and failed the vet, which was the only reason I could afford him at that time. However, his condition did not prevent him from teaching me, and subsequently many of my pupils, the 'feel' of lateral work, and this enabed me to go on and teach my other school horses at that time to perform the exercises, too. I was amazed at the effects that lateral work could achieve, in aiding not only collection but also straightness.

There are still various schools of thought on when to introduce lateral work, and also whether it should be carried out in walk or trot, but I have an open mind about it.

- Certain horses are so sensitive to sideways movement, and will move away from the leg very easily, that I would introduce it very early in their training, but only in walk.

- The Portuguese use a lot of lateral exercises in walk, not only at the beginning of training but also later, as their main warm-up regime.

- Other trainers of the German school would not agree with using lateral steps in walk. There are some who say that it ruins a horse's walk, but I have never found this to be the case. The quickest way to ruin a horse's walk is to try to collect him too early when working on a straight line, or even on a circle: it is all too easy for the horse to lose the clear, four-beat rhythm of the walk and for it to become two-time.

- Some would argue that lateral work should be used only to increase collection, but I disagree. It has many uses in its simpler forms, which can then be honed to perfection as the horse's strength and depth of education increases.

When teaching the horse any lateral exercise, remember that it takes the learning horse longer to cross his legs than it does to walk in a straight line. Give him time to sort his legs out, and ask for no more than a few steps at a time.

Rhythm is still all-important, and although it will have to be sacrificed for a short time, until the horse is able to take a few steps in the required position and at the necessary angle, the immediate priority once this is achieved must be to re-establish the normal rhythm and tempo. Only when these are re-established will it be possible to glide effortlessly sideways, maintaining the angle, increasing the step under with the hindlegs and the lightening of the forehand, and amplifying the sweep and expression that is desirable in all lateral movement.

Let us look at the various lateral exercises that can be performed. I have included turn on the forehand and leg yielding, which some may not view as Classical, but I feel that they have their uses, for reasons which we will examine.

TURN ON THE FOREHAND

This movement has often been castigated by dressage trainers, because it is a stationary movement which does not encourage engagement of the hindlegs. Some will include its use in schooling, providing that the horse is allowed to move forwards again on completion of the turn. I have no problem with this, but I really do think that people can become too pedantic about certain things that are purely a means to an end – and this is one of them.

The turn on the forehand has practical uses out hacking, such as for opening gates from the back of the horse. For the everyday rider, who takes her horse out into the countryside and does not merely bore him by endless hours of exercises in the school, the movement has its place in the horse's education. I use it for this purpose, but initially to teach the horse that when I increase the pressure of one leg, I wish him to move away from it.

TEACHING THE HORSE

To start with the turn on the forehand can be practised with the horse facing the school wall or fence, so blocking his forward movement; nor should he be allowed to move backwards (if he tries I send him forwards by closing my legs). He then soon realizes that you wish him to move his hindquarters around, so that he returns to the track alongside the wall. For the first few times, I do not worry about sending the horse forward again immediately after the turn has been accomplished. I praise him if he has made a reasonable attempt at it, and then let him walk forwards, before trying the turn again.

As we saw in Chapter 6 it is very important that the rider's leg is not used with a solid pressure. Far from moving away from it, the horse will try to push back against it, which is his instinct. Instead, in *all* lateral work, you should use the leg in a regular series of nudges, by contracting and releasing the calf muscles – *not* by bringing the leg away and tapping with it. I much prefer to reinforce the action of the

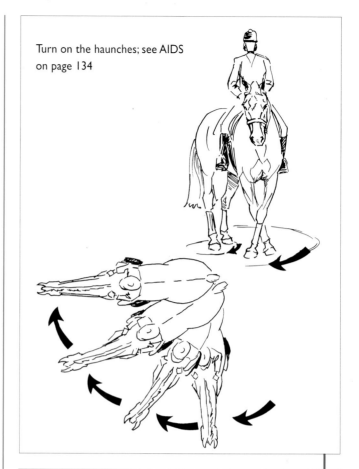

Turn on the haunches; see AIDS on page 134

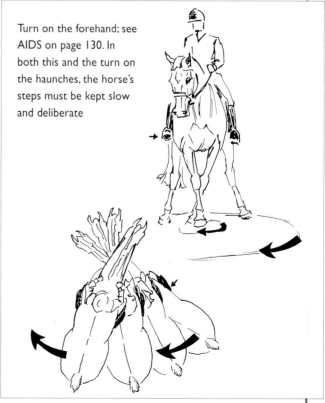

Turn on the forehand; see AIDS on page 130. In both this and the turn on the haunches, the horse's steps must be kept slow and deliberate

Moon practising leg yield

leg with a tap of the dressage whip, so that the horse learns to go from light leg aids from the beginning.

If the horse really doesn't understand what is required of him, it can be helpful to have an assistant on the ground who can lightly push the hindquarters over as the rider uses her leg. Again, the pressure should not be solid, the assistant pushing and then decreasing the pressure, and repeating the process until the horse takes the desired step sideways. Always reward by releasing the leg aid and praising the horse the instant that this occurs. Dispense with the assistant as soon as the horse understands and begins to move around away from the pressure of the leg alone, aided by the whip if necessary. The horse should not be allowed to move so fast that he pivots around his inside foreleg; each step must be slow and deliberate so that the forelegs describe a very small circle. As soon as the horse is completing a 90 degree turn with ease, he should be made to walk forward again, stepping purposefully through the transition from the turn to the first stride of walk.

THE AIDS

To ride a turn on the forehand, ride the horse forward across the school and halt facing the wall. Raise your inside hand a little, squeezing the rein to flex the horse's jaw and turn the head to the inside just enough to see the inside eye and nostril. Use the outside rein to control any desire to move forwards, by closing your fingers firmly around the rein. Bring your inside leg back just behind the girth, and apply pressure, then release, press again, then release, in rhythm with the steps of the horse until he has completed the turn. The outside leg remains in place, and is lightly pressed against the horse's side.

LEG YIELDING

Leg yielding is almost self-explanatory, in that the horse does just that – yields to pressure from the leg and moves sideways away from it. The horse's head

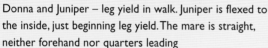

Donna and Juniper – leg yield in walk. Juniper is flexed to the inside, just beginning leg yield. The mare is straight, neither forehand nor quarters leading

Donna and Juniper showing good lateral crossing in walk leg yield. Donna needs to have her outside rein in contact with Juniper's neck, acting as a barrier to stop any tendency to 'dive' through her outside shoulder – a common tendency with horses, particularly when learning leg yield

and neck are flexed very slightly to the inside, with the horse moving away from the direction of the bend – so, for example, if the horse is flexed to the right, his body will be moving to the left. The horse should move parallel to the wall of the school, with neither his forehand nor his quarters leading.

This is the easiest of all the lateral exercises for the horse to perform. Some trainers will not teach it, because they feel that it can confuse the horse when he begins the half pass, where he is *flexed towards* and *moving in* the same direction. I have never found any confusion, unless the rider has curved the horse excessively to the inside and has unwittingly been allowing him to escape through his outside shoulder,

because there has been too much bend in the neck.

If we train the horse to perform this exercise correctly, it is a simple and effective way of gaining early sideways movement. Unlike the half pass, leg yielding does not require a lot of effort on the part of the horse. In half pass, because the horse is bent into the direction of the movement, the outside shoulder and neck muscles on that side have to stretch quite considerably in order to gain the required sideways sweep of the outside foreleg. In leg yielding, because the horse is flexed slightly away from the direction of the movement, there is no stretching of the neck and shoulder muscles, as it is the inside foreleg which is crossing over.

Here Donna has a little too much bend in Juniper's neck, which will encourage her to drift through her outside shoulder – it hasn't happened but it could easily within the next few strides

Front/threequarter sideways view, showing right hindleg crossing over, and Donna's leg positioned a little back (toe sticking out though!)

THE AIDS

Inside rein flexes horse to inside so that eye and nostril are visible to rider.

Inside leg, a little behind the girth, is used in time with the stride, as the belly swings to the outside.

Outside rein, acting passively against the neck. Outside leg in normal place assists impulsion.

TEACHING THE HORSE

In the school, I like to start to teach the exercise from the quarter line, as the horse's natural inclination is to move back to the track. The only trouble is that sometimes the desire to return to the track is all too strong, and so the horse tries to hurry, taking short,

quick little strides and escaping outwards through his shoulder, while bending too strongly at the base of the neck.

This is where the use of the outside rein comes in, to prevent this from happening. When any horse has this tendency, you must block him at the base of the neck bringing your outside hand into contact with it, the rein lying along the length of the neck to act as a barrier, which prevents the horse from diving back to the track with his shoulder leading. Press the outside rein firmly along the neck, and if necessary, purely as a remedial measure, open the inside rein, and apply strong pressure with the outside leg behind the girth, sending the horse forward again with the

Leg yield in trot. Juniper really crossing, reaching well over with outside shoulder. This time, Donna is correctly using her outside rein so that the inside rein is very light. Juniper is flexing beautifully to the inside with just a vibration of the fingers on the inside rein. The next stage is to start teaching half pass; she can already produce good shoulder-in and travers

Here I've deliberately asked Jo to use a strong inside hand, so that Max is bending at the base of the neck, with his forehand clearly in advance of his quarters, 'falling through his outside shoulder'

Here, Jo has brought the outside rein into contact to lie along Max's neck, acting as a barrier to prevent the outward drift, and must also bring her inside hand out – not back! – to bring the whole forehand back into line …

inside leg at the girth. This straightens him again and prevents him being able to scoot back to the track through his outside shoulder. Repeat the exercise, always rewarding the horse as soon as he makes the correct angle.

Once the horse has fully understood the meaning of the increased pressure of one leg, I tend not to practise the above two exercises again, except in practical applications when hacking out.

TURN ON THE HAUNCHES

I usually teach this exercise next, as it is particularly useful for gaining control of the forehand by means of the outside rein. All horses are sensitive to this use of the outside rein, and require little teaching in order to understand its meaning.

THE AIDS

Ride the horse along the track on the long side of the school and halt. Maintaining the closed seat to

prevent the horse from moving forwards, vibrate the outside rein against the neck, flexing the horse to the inside with the fingers of your inside hand, your outside leg behind the girth and inside leg at the girth. The horse should not pivot on the inside hind foot, but should pick it up and place it down again at each step, making as small a circle as possible. As in turn on the forehand, do not allow him to step round too quickly, causing him to pivot. Make the steps slow and deliberate at first – give him time to complete each step.

TEACHING THE HORSE

At this early stage, I am satisfied with the horse making a quarter circle; I then return to the track in leg yield. As soon as the horse is able to make this quarter turn with ease, I ask for the remaining steps to be made in the same manner, so that a complete half-turn is achieved. Some would say that this is too early to teach the turn on the haunches, but I beg to differ: all lateral work is so much easier when the horse is

… as in this photo

In this shot, Max is starting to straighten, forehand coming back in, and quarters nearly in line. I would ride straight forward for a few steps, then restart the leg yield

truly conversant with the meaning and application of the outside rein.

Make sure that your outside leg acts with firm pressure behind the girth at each step, to bring the outside of the horse around, and prevent him from crossing his hindlegs over and turning like a boat at anchor.

SHOULDER-IN

This is probably the most useful exercise ever invented for suppling, collecting and straightening the horse. There are several schools of thought on the way in which it should be ridden, but I tend to stick to what I know has worked for me when riding many different horses, regardless of how they have been schooled.

There are several different degrees of shoulder-in:
■ We begin by teaching the horse the small degree of shoulder-in known as 'shoulder-fore', by merely asking him to move his forehand very slightly to the inside.

■ The next degree of shoulder-in is the three-track version, where the horse makes three distinctly visible tracks in the school surface. The forehand is displaced to the inside track, the forelegs crossing over, while the hindlegs, with the inside hind stepping well under, do not cross but move as normal along the track. In this version, the horse makes an angle of 30 degrees to the wall. Viewed from the front, when the movement is carried out correctly you can see clearly that the outside hindleg makes one track, the outside fore and inside hind on the same line make the second track, and the inside foreleg makes the third.

■ When the horse has achieved a high degree of suppleness and collection, shoulder-in may be ridden as a four-track movement. The horse, very well engaged and bent around the rider's inside leg, crosses all four legs and is at an angle roughly 45 degrees to the wall. Unfortunately, at lower levels of dressage four track shoulder-ins are all too common, because the rider, forgetting to apply the outside leg behind the girth and concentrating too much on the inside rein, is allowing the horse to escape through his quarters, so that the hindlegs do cross. Due to the lack of bend and engagement of the inside hindleg, performed in this way the exercise is merely a leg yield along the wall, and will contribute neither to straightening nor collection.

Shoulder-fore – very small degree of shoulder-in – first stage of learning the movement – inside hind and outside fore making one track, slight bend to inside

THE AIDS

There is some divergence of opinion as to the aids for shoulder-in, but I teach what Desi Lorent taught me, partly because it always works but also because it is entirely logical. Most schools of thought teach the same aids for shoulder-in as for turning and circling. This to me seems distinctly *illogical*, because it can lead only to confusion on the part of the horse – and, to my mind, is also the reason why the exercise is often so badly performed.

When the rider uses the turning aids to perform shoulder-in, she has to reinforce them, with the inside hand predominating, so that the horse bends at the base of the neck and not from behind the shoulder.

Shoulder-in on three tracks at 30° to the wall

This, in turn, results in the rider having to use more outside rein to control any excessive bend. Likewise, because the horse's neck has bent too much to the inside, the quarters are liable to swing out – rather as a boat would at anchor – so that the rider then has to use more outside leg to prevent this from happening. The whole affair turns into a struggle, when instead it should flow without apparent effort on the part of either horse or rider. When, on the other hand, you teach the horse a set of aids which is different from those used to turn, he understands very easily and stronger aids are unnecessary. One set means one thing, another set something completely different. Logical? The horse seems to think so!

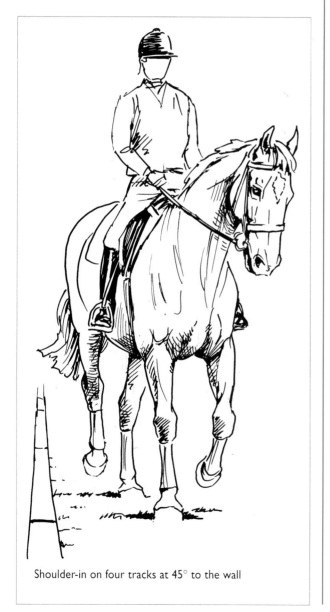

Shoulder-in on four tracks at 45° to the wall

Aids for turning: recap

We examined the aids for turning in detail on pages 86–92, but need to recap briefly for our purposes here. The aids normally taught for turning are inside rein asking for the inside bend, with inside leg applied at the girth to keep the inside hindleg stepping under, and outside rein restricting and controlling the bend, with outside leg applied behind the girth to prevent the quarters from swinging outwards. The rider's shoulders turn to the inside to mirror those of the horse.

In contrast, I teach aids which work biomechanically with the horse and which I find every horse reacts to immediately, regardless of previous schooling. The rider advances the inside hip slightly, by pointing it in the direction of the turn and in so doing should feel more weight concentrated on the inside seatbone. The inside hand is raised slightly, with the fingers squeezing or vibrating the rein to flex the horse to the inside, so that the inside eye and nostril are visible from the saddle. The outside hand, lowered against the base of the neck, acts passively as a barrier to prevent the horse from drifting outwards, while the outside leg, applied just behind the girth, controls the swing of the quarters. The rider's shoulders do nothing, simply following the line made by the hips as the inside hip is advanced. The outside shoulder may appear to be very slightly back, in line with the outside hip, but is not deliberately placed so by the rider, which would exaggerate the line instead of allowing it to happen naturally.

Logical aids for shoulder-in

For shoulder-in, I teach the aids that others use for turning. Because it is the horse's outside shoulder which leads in shoulder-in, the rider's shoulders need to turn *slightly* to the inside, so that the outside hip points down the track in the direction of the movement. Remember, however, that the hips must not be fixed and immobile, which would block the horse's forward movement, but must still dip and rise with the undulations of the horse's back, the outside hip advancing with the horse's outside shoulder. Many riders concentrate so hard on the rest of the aids that they sit stock still – and then wonder why the horse does not move either! The seat should not, however, make an exaggerated diagonal slide in the saddle at each stride. Some riders appear to be trying physically to push the horse sideways with their own seat.

The inside hand, again raised slightly, flexes the horse to the inside, while the outside hand, lowered, this time used actively, vibrates lightly against the neck to initiate displacement of the shoulders to the inside: provided the angle is maintained it then remains passively lowered against the horse's neck. The inside leg acts in time with the swing of the belly at the girth (not behind it as is so often seen, which is the prime cause of 'leg yield along the wall') to encourage the inside hind to step further under, thereby increasing collection and lightening the forehand. The outside leg remains behind the girth, acting passively as a barrier, or actively if the horse has a tendency to swing the quarters out on that rein. Because the turn of the rider's shoulders is only slight there should be no danger of outside heel coming up, as there is when most riders use this aid, inadvisably, for turning.

TEACHING THE HORSE

Most trainers teach the horse a few steps of shoulder-in by performing a small (say, 10m) circle in the corner of the school and then continuing the bend out of the circle, by holding the horse in the shoulder-in position and carrying on down the track for a few strides. I do not use this method. Because I like to use the two separate sets of aids for turning and shoulder-in, I prefer to execute a fairly deep corner, ensuring that the horse steps well under with the inside hindleg throughout the quarter circle of the corner; then, just as I come out of the corner, I switch my aids, without abruptness, and the horse nearly always moves easily forwards for a few steps in shoulder-fore, without the need to hold him into the angle as happens if you normally use the same aids for turning. I am satisfied with even three good steps, and praise the horse immediately. By building gradually on this beginning, with a few more steps performed at a time, after a few schooling sessions most horses will be gliding easily in shoulder-fore down the full length of the school.

At this stage I will introduce the exercise in trot, again gradually, until the horse is once more performing shoulder-fore with ease down the full length of the school. Once the horse is established in this, I will start to ask for a little more bend and angle, until the full three-track, 30-degree shoulder-in is achieved. Later, at a much more advanced stage, as the horse is rendered more and more supple by the work, I would introduce a deeper bend and angle of 45

degrees. Shoulder-in may also be performed in canter.

In time, you will find that the horse becomes so sensitive that the hand and leg aids become mere whispers, the weight being the predominant – and of course, invisible – signal to the horse. My own Arabian stallion will proceed down the track in shoulder-in if I simply turn my shoulders to the inside; if I then advance my inside hip, he will immediately turn off the track across the school. To the onlooker, I appear to have done nothing.

I prefer to teach shoulder-in – and indeed all other lateral exercises – in walk to begin with. In accordance with Portuguese Classical teaching, I will also continue to use this work in walk throughout the training of all horses, more so with some than with others, depending upon breed or type. I find that the short-backed breeds, typically Iberian and some of our native breeds, or any horse that is close coupled benefits particularly from lateral work in walk. Generally the longer-backed Warmblood and Thoroughbred types find lateral work easier, and it is best to move on to more work in trot to develop a deeper lateral bend.

TRAVERS AND RENVERS

Travers is an exercise that prepares the horse for half pass. It can be performed along the wall, across the diagonal or down the centre line.

In travers, the horse is bent slightly around the rider's inside leg, and moves in the direction of the bend, with the quarters brought to the inside track so that the horse is making an angle of about 30 degrees to the track. This angle can be made deeper at a later stage in training, when I would ask for about 45 degrees, making the movement four-track instead of three-track. A three-track travers is the same angle as a shoulder-in with the horse's head to the wall; the four-track version is a half pass along the wall.

A lot of riders get confused between travers and its cousin renvers, but the difference is really quite simple: in renvers, the horse is again bent around the rider's inside leg, but this time his quarters remain on the track and his forehand is brought to the inside. I find that renvers is the most difficult of the lateral exercises for the horse to perform when first learning the work. Depending entirely upon the aptitude of the individual, I will often leave this exercise until last, teaching half pass first. Once the horse is established in half pass, renvers is never a problem.

THE AIDS, AND TEACHING THE HORSE

When teaching the horse travers, it is easier to start from a corner of the school, in walk. The horse is already flexed to the inside, with the rider's inside hand raised a little and the fingers squeezing or vibrating on the rein. The outside hand vibrates against the neck for just the first few strides and then remains in the passive position, to ask the horse to move his forehand sideways. The outside leg acts behind the girth, increasing the pressure – as always, in the rhythm of the stride (a solid, unvarying push) – so that the horse moves his quarters over on to the inside track, while the inside leg maintains impulsion at the girth. In travers, renvers and half pass, it is the horse's outside hindleg which is the main source of sideways propulsion, but as the movement is both sideways and forwards, the inside hindleg is equally important to create the forward impetus. As with shoulder-in, the rider must remember to move with the horse, this time advancing the inside hip in time with the advancing of the horse's inside shoulder.

As with shoulder-in, be satisfied with just a few correct steps, and build up gradually until the horse is capable of maintaining the travers position along the full length of the school, before beginning work in

Travers; the horse is bent slightly around the rider's *inside* leg, with his quarters brought to the inside track

Renvers; the horse is bent slightly around the rider's *inside* leg, his quarters remaining on the track

Woody showing 30° travers, slightly flexed to right, left hind and right fore making one track

Travers from behind – horse flexed to right and moving quarters in to right

Woody, just learning half-pass. Debbie has begun the exercise in travers on the diagonal, and is now pushing his quarters over until the movement becomes a half-pass

At this stage, when learning half-pass, I do not mind if the forehand leads slightly. The Spanish Riding School ride half-pass in this way, but in competition the horse's body must be parallel to the long side of the school. He is not yet crossing his legs in an extravagant sideways sweep. As he develops more strength in his hindquarters and stretch in his shoulder muscles, and a deeper lateral bend, the movement will be more expressive

Already Woody is beginning to develop more 'sweep' sideways – note how right hindleg is engaged and left shoulder is stretching sideways

trot. Renvers and travers may also be performed in canter, and are particularly useful as a preparation for the canter pirouette.

In renvers – say, on the right rein – the horse proceeds along the wall with his quarters on the track, forehand brought to the inside and is flexed to the left. The movement is really no more than an inverted travers, but I find that it is not as easy to teach to the horse, because you do not have the help of the corner to guide him into the bend. In travers the curve of the corner is continued, whereas in renvers the bend has to be reversed. In my experience, it is best to allow the horse to straighten for a couple of strides after the corner, and then to ask for renvers using the same aids as for travers, but positioning the horse approximately.

HALF PASS

Of all the lateral movements, half pass – when seen in its finished, advanced form – is certainly the most beautiful. I will never forget Olympic champion Rembrandt's breathtaking half passes at the pinnacle of his career, where he gained an enormous amount of ground as he swept sideways, still maintaining the spring and expression in his stride whether at trot or canter, always totally symmetrical and wonderfully light.

Not all horses can aspire to attain so much impulsion and freedom of the shoulders, but I am certain that we would see far more examples of superior lateral work if only horses were given the freedom to move, without the restraints imposed upon them by their riders. If the horse is pulled in at the front end on a tight contact, so that the muscles of the neck are contracted back into its base, the shoulders will be tight and unable to sweep sideways to their maximum extent. When the contact is light and the horse is in self-carriage, then the forehand will be free to move to the best of its ability.

THE AIDS

The aids for half pass are the same as for travers and renvers. The inside hand flexes the horse to the inside, just sufficiently for the rider to see the inside eye and nostril, and the outside hand again vibrates or presses against the neck to instruct the horse to move his forehand over. The outside leg, acting behind the girth, moves the quarters sideways, while the inside leg maintains the impulsion necessary to carry the whole horse forwards and sideways with lightness and expression.

TEACHING THE HORSE

In competition dressage, half pass is ridden with the horse almost parallel to the wall of the school. The Spanish Riding School, however, ride half pass with the forehand leading at a more oblique angle to the wall. When teaching horses half pass, I use the Spanish Riding School version to make things a little easier to start with, gradually bringing the quarters over until the parallel position is reached.

Starting across the diagonal in travers and finishing with the last few strides in half pass is a popular method with some eminent trainers, as is going into shoulder-in for a few strides out of the corner before commencing half pass across the diagonal, and I have no quarrel with either. Options are always needed, because every horse is different.

RIDER CO-ORDINATION

Most riders experience some difficulty in learning lateral work. There seems to be so much to think about! The problem is that (particularly in the UK) horse and rider are often learning together, due to the lack of schoolmasters in many riding establishments. On the Continent, schoolmasters are freely available for riders to learn on, which helps a great deal. A good schoolmaster horse that will only perform a movement if the rider gets it right, is the most valuable asset a riding school can have. The rider quickly develops the feel for sideways movement, and can then recognize when their own horse gets it right or wrong.

I find that the most common rider error in lateral work is to use too much inside hand, and a tight, restrictive outside rein, so that the horse bends at the base of the neck instead of from behind the shoulder. In most instances, this is because the rider has not been taught to raise the inside hand and vibrate the fingers, or the correct use of the outside rein. Raising

Some horses find lateral work as easy as falling off a log, others need a little time before the idea takes root. The former are usually very light, sensitive rides in all respects, and often find going sideways rather exciting to begin with. This does not always mean that such horses are of hot-blooded descent, as I discovered when teaching lateral work to the part-Percheron show cob that I competed at county level a couple of years ago. She became so enthusiastic about it that her first attempts at sideways steps usually included a few 'airs above the ground' that would not have been out of place at the Spanish Riding School! As soon as she realized that the work was not really that exciting, she settled down and took it all in her stride.

Likewise, my Lipizzaner gelding also went through the repertoire of his illustrious sire and cousins in Vienna, before deciding that this 'sideways stuff' was not quite so intoxicating after all. The most important thing of all is that you do not lose your patience throughout these fizzy moments. Sitting quietly and firmly, and then resuming what you had asked for, is always vastly more effective than beating a horse into submission. I am certain that, with my Lipizzaner in particular, had I lost my temper and hit him, I would have ended up on the floor on a daily basis in the earlier stages of his schooling. Now, while he has retained his sense of humour, he is a delightful, highly responsive ride, who will go sideways with the lightest of leg aids – and no 'airs above the ground' either!

Left: Nicole Uphoff-Becker on Rembrandt, showing half pass

Right: Jenny Key on Flame showing the aids for half pass: left leg behind the girth, left rein against the neck. Jenny is flexing the mare to the right, and she is moving right

the inside hand – never more than an inch or two – prevents it from wanting to pull back, which it does mostly from habit, but often also due to lack of correction on the part of the instructor.

Once the rider is at ease with the aids for lateral movement, everything else seems to fall into place. I can still remember how, many years ago when I was first learning lateral exercises, my feel and timing seemed to take on a new dimension. The horse's legs did indeed feel as if they had become my own, and all other work seemed to flow more smoothly.

EQUINE APTITUDE

Nearly all horses, regardless of breed or type, should be quite capable of performing lateral work – perhaps not always with the degree of sideways sweep or expression to be found in horses that are of ideal conformation, but sufficiently accurate in execution to warrant a reasonable mark in a dressage test. Sadly, however, not all judges take breed and type into account, and, regardless of whether the horse is carrying out the exercise to the best of its ability or limitations, will mark it below an extravagant mover whose work is less correct.

Whatever your horse's type or breeding, do not be put off trying to school him to a decent level. I first met Jenny at a dressage festival a few years ago. I had been despairing of the standard of riding, when a magnificent and very large horse came out from the horsebox lines. I was immediately impressed with how quietly his small lady rider sat, and the correctness of his way of going. I watched her ride her test, which she won easily, and remarked on what a pleasure it had been to watch her ride. Later she brought out Flame, the mare featured in these photographs, and we chatted whilst she worked her in. We have remained in touch as friends, and Jenny is, in my opinion, one of the most talented dressage riders and trainers in the country; she deserves far more recognition than she gets.

Jenny riding Flame, her homebred TB Grand Prix mare

Above: Flame has great talent for piaffe and passage

Below: Jenny and Flame executing a flying change

Occasionally, a conformation fault may cause a horse to be marked down because it moves in a not entirely conventional manner. A friend, Jenny Key, has trained her homebred Thoroughbred mare to Grand Prix level. Jenny is very talented, having schooled the mare with minimal help, visiting a top trainer for a few days just a couple of times a year. The mare moves very wide in front, her forelegs splaying out to the side and making a 'V' shape. In half pass, this means that she is unable to cross her forelegs to any great degree, yet gains a great deal of sideways ground in every step. Despite the fact that the necessary impulsion is quite obviously present, and the forehand is truly light, many judges have consistently marked her down. Her rider has performed a remarkable feat in training her to the highest level yet only a very small minority of judges have recognized the correctness of the work. In spite of the slightly strange movement – which, in any case, is only visible when viewed from the front – the overall picture is very light and aesthetically pleasing, with horse and rider unmistakably a real partnership.

Jenny and Flame executing half pass, showing good lateral bend and 'sideways sweep', despite the mare's foreleg conformation

12 THE CLASSICAL PATH – RIDING IN LIGHTNESS

In Chapter 6 we looked briefly at the use of the seat. In fact, the use of the seat as the ultimate, invisible aid to collection is the key to lightness in the horse.

For me, 'lightness' is when the horse, at whatever stage in his training, accepts and responds to the aids without force needing to be applied. The highest level of lightness occurs when the horse will work in complete self-carriage, his hindquarters fully engaged, on reins that have no tension, the merest vibration of the fingers being sufficient to communicate the rider's wishes to the horse. When they first sit on a horse that will go in this manner, many riders do not like it. They feel insecure, because they are so used to the reins being the primary source of control, as a steering and stopping device. To me, it is the most marvellous feeling in the world. I do not compete my horses in competition dressage tests, because I know that if I rode them in this way, with *semi-slack reins*, I would be marked down for insufficient contact. I have even heard one top judge remark that the horse cannot possibly be 'on the bit' if the reins are not taut. I disagree! With a few notable exceptions, many of even the top competition dressage horses in the world today have never reached the stage of collection that

There are many Iberian riders who still ride and train in this way, because it is the traditional one. They do not seem to have found it necessary to 'improve' on the Classical methods. While the Iberian horses are perhaps not as powerful in their ability to extend as the Warmblood, they are purpose-bred for collection and can 'sit' with ease, raising the forehand and producing this true lightness that comes from correct training into collection. Up to now, any rider who trained an Iberian horse intending to compete would have been laughed out of the arena at the higher levels.

permits the horse to achieve this supreme degree of lightness and balance.

At last, these horses are becoming acceptable, but on the evidence so far it seems that the temptation is to train them in the competition manner, resulting in loss of the lightness that has been so highly prized in their way of going throughout the history of Classical equitation.

Emperador, Julian Marczak's Andalucian stallion, showing the lightness typical of the breed. The ability of Iberian horses to compete at higher levels has only recently been recognized

ENLIGHTENED EQUITATION

To use such a subtle application of the seat as the unilateral tightening of the seat/thigh muscles as the ultimate aid to lightness, the rider must first have developed good basic 'feel' before trying to use, in order not to mis-time the aid and confuse the horse. In this instance, it is not easy to talk the reader through step-by-step as every horse is so different, and the rider must time and co-ordinate the aids according to the moment. This can only really be learned by trial and error, preferably riding schoolmasters who will only respond when the right amount of the aid is applied, at the right time.

When the seat rather than the hands is used as a collecting and retarding aid, the horse is free to express himself. So many riders seem to think that reeling in the front end of the horse, thereby shortening the steps, is collection. This is *contraction*! The horse is concertinaed into a bow shape through force, thereby restricting the use of his body and the flexion of his joints. Instead, when the seat is used to 'lift' the horse's back and slow the pace, while the rider's legs continue to encourage the hindlegs to step under, greater spring is engendered. The more attuned the horse is to the use of the seat, the more subtle the aid can be. The rider eventually becomes so accustomed to the use of the seat over the hands, that the latter can sometimes seem surplus to requirements! The horse, unrestricted by the force of the hand, grows prouder and more confident in his movement, offering the lightness, cadence and expression that is the hallmark of Classical equitation.

I have already mentioned the great maestro, Nuño Oliveira. He was without doubt the greatest rider that I have ever seen. At 66 years of age, his passing some years ago came all too soon. With the significant move now taking place towards Classical equitation, if he were alive today he would no doubt have been in even greater demand as a teacher worldwide. Sadly for other riders, he was a very private man, and not nearly enough people were able to witness his horsemanship. As I have also mentioned, I was privileged to watch him ride when he gave displays at the 1966 Horse of the Year Show. Aged 13, I sat electrified by the art being enacted before me. I knew, there and then, that this was how I wanted to ride. Few, if any, have the talent, or the time, to aspire to reach his level, but to learn to ride with lightness and harmony, rather than force, even at the lower levels, is an achievable goal for any rider.

In order to overcome the obstacles that lie in the path of 'Enlightened Equitation', you have to be brave, and unafraid to stand up for what you instinctively feel is right. Many students think that just because an instructor has impressive-sounding qualifications, then she must be right. If she is making you ride your horse with force or violence, don't put up with it! After all, it is not you who are the recipient of the abuse, but your horse. Most people profess to love their horses, and yet I have seen them, under instruction, hitting them until welts stood out on the shoulders and flanks. This, of course, was deemed quite acceptable, because the trainer had told them to do it.

> To prove that strength is not the answer, I will use the illustrator of this book as an example! Dianne Breeze is one of the quietest and most stylish riders I have seen in the UK. She is slightly built, and probably no more than 1.65m (5ft 5in) in height. Her Prix St George horse, which she has trained from a novice, is a strapping Dutch chap of 17 hands or more. Watching Dianne ride him is a delight, as she sits with ease to his big movement, her aids all but invisible. I have been privileged to use this partnership in one of my lecture demonstrations, and I could have had no better models to prove that even with a small lady on a very big horse, there need be no power struggle – just total harmony.

Why is it that riders seem oblivious to the fact that such actions cause the horse pain? Do we become so inured to their feelings, simply because we have to pay for their keep and attend to their every need, and expect that in return the horse should accept whatever we do to them under saddle, without question? Is this fair treatment? So many horses' characters are maligned, simply because they are misunderstood.

If somebody asks me to do something, I will usually do it, but if someone orders me to do a particular task, I am unlikely to do it willingly, if at all! I doubt that I would have been a very good candidate for army training. Most horses are the same. Ask them

Dianne Breeze (see box above) on Political Princess

One mare that I worked with on a clinic stands out in my memory. A quality sort, mostly Thoroughbred, with excellent conformation, she had a reputation for being ungenerous. This did not mean that she had vices, such as bucking or rearing, merely that she was not easy to school, being resistant to the bit and tending to go above it, very much on her forehand in canter and with a generally cross expression. Her rider had owned her for six years, the mare now being ten, and had managed to do some dressage with her at Preliminary level, but had ceased to progress any further, despite regular lessons with the resident dressage trainer at the livery yard where she was stabled.

A top Grand Prix rider/trainer had begun to take clinics at the yard, and the pair had joined in one of them. The trainer had ridden the horse with considerable force, until she was sweating all over and he likewise, in his efforts to bend her to his will. He had then dismounted and, like others before, had pronounced her 'ungenerous'.

During my clinic, I also rode the mare. Sure enough, in the snaffle she was resistant and heavy, and very much on her forehand in canter. I changed the bit to my old favourite, the rubber pelham. Instantly, her expression softened. I asked with my fingers for her to relax her jaw and, even with very light squeezing on the rein, she responded in seconds. Over the next 40 minutes, I only had to ask her a few times with my fingers, used ever more lightly, for her jaw to remain relaxed and her head correctly placed without any intervention on my part. Within a few circuits of the school, the mare started to swing through her back and her stride became longer and more powerful; by now my fingers were not even closed around the reins, so light had she become.

I have seldom ridden a horse that complied so instantly with everything I asked. I worked her through transitions from halt to walk and vice versa: her response to my seat aid was immediate. We progressed to halt-trot and trot-halt transitions, the trot becoming lighter and springier by the minute. I asked her owner whether the mare had ever done any lateral work, to which she replied that she hadn't. I asked the mare for shoulder-in in walk, which she managed very easily. I then tried a little travers, also in walk, and she found this very easy too. I then tried both in trot and she glided smoothly along the wall in both exercises, as if she had been doing this work for years.

I could not resist trying a little half pass, which she also managed with ease. It would have taken comparatively little time for her lateral work to be exceptional. Her canter needed some work on, so we set about using many transitions from trot to canter and back. I tried walk to canter and she popped up into it with ease, returning to walk with a squeeze of my seat and thigh muscles, and almost no tension on the reins at all. Within a few minutes, she was cantering in perfect balance, wonderfully 'uphill', and I can only describe the feeling as like sitting on clouds. I also could not resist trying a flying change. Although a little 'late behind', this too was accomplished. By this time, the mare's owner, and other livery clients who were also on the clinic, were sitting in the gallery with mouths agape!

Reluctantly, I handed the mare back to her rider. I told her that far from being 'ungenerous', she was one of the most *generous and talented horses that I have ever been privileged to sit on. Her owner remarked that the mare had looked like a dressage schoolmaster. I replied that she was, if you* allowed *her to be! Provided that she understood what was asked, she gave everything, and you can ask for no more than that. I felt almost sorry for the Grand Prix trainer who had dismissed her out of hand. What a ride he had missed! If only he had worked* with, *not* against, *the horse, he would have had a ride made in heaven. I wish that she had been for sale, because she would have been here in my stable right now.*

Merely changing the bit to one whose action the mare felt comfortable with and which required no force, just the light, yielding pressure of my fingers activating the curb chain, initiated the relaxation of her lower jaw. Then, by applying aids that work biomechanically with the horse's body, the mare understood easily and gladly carried out all that was asked of her. You will note that I use the word 'asked', not 'demanded', because had I attempted to use force I would have achieved nothing, especially with a horse who is patently highly intelligent and does not suffer fools gladly.

in a way that they understand, and most will happily comply with our requests. Demand, through force and strength, in a way that causes discomfort or even pain, and resistance and evasion will inevitably be provoked.

HORSES FOR COURSES

I am not against competition *per se*, but I do think that it can change people. I myself have seen this many times. Nuño Oliveira only ever competed a couple of times in his lifetime, and even then against his better judgement. He trained purely for his own sense of achievement and pleasure, not to be judged better than others. I know of many riders who without the challenge of competition would never get on a horse again. They do not ride for the pleasure of owning horses, but solely to go out to a show and beat the rest. Sadly, I have seen many who, if they do *not* beat the rest, beat the horse instead.

There are horses whose character is such that they cannot resist trying out their trainer's patience by throwing in a few 'equibatics', as I term them, for good measure. There are a few horses whose nature is not as generous as others, and who will only perform grudgingly, despite kind ownership and training. I have occasionally had to deal with a genuinely mean-spirited horse, whose background has been known from birth and who has never had to withstand mistreatment yet still will not give willingly of himself. These horses rarely, if ever, give in.

In a few cases, it is physical limitations caused by faulty conformation that make the rider's chosen discipline unsuitable for the horse, with the result that he shows his unhappiness through truculence. In such instances, it is essential that the rider tries to find a different occupation for the horse, either by switching disciplines herself, or by selling the horse to an owner who wants him for a different purpose.

Try, therefore, to choose a horse with the conformation, temperament and aptitude for the job you require him to do.

RESISTANCE THROUGH PAIN

Like all sports, riding has its ups and downs. Nothing is ever perfect. Even the greatest riders have their moments of disaster, as well as their triumphs. When a living animal, with a mind and will of its own, is your partner in sport, rather than a machine, a bat or a racquet, the odds that a few differences of opinion may arise are somewhat shortened! When this occurs, *never* lose your temper, however great the temptation. Always analyse the situation and try to imagine what your horse may be feeling – put yourself in his place. If you suspect that any resistance may be due to pain, have him checked by your vet. If he is evading the bit, despite your putting into practise the methods I have described in this book, get a reputable equine dentist to make certain that his teeth are not sharp.

Always ask a dentist whether he uses a proper ratchet gag; this is the only way he can reach the back teeth, which are often missed. I had a big Thoroughbred ex-racehorse in my yard a few years ago, who had had his teeth rasped by the vet only three months previously. He was still very fidgety in his mouth, despite our trying several very mild bits, including my beloved pelham. Although he went best in this, he was really not at all settled.

I heard that a very well-known equine dentist was in the area, and I asked him to treat the horse. Having felt around in the horse's mouth, he produced an instrument that looked like a pair of bolt croppers. He then asked me to put my hand into the horse's mouth and feel for myself the sharp points on the back teeth. The dentist then chopped off the points, which

---

I know of one horse whose owner really wants to do dressage. The horse is rather croup high, and ill-conformed to do dressage at anything other than the lower levels. He is possessed of a rather sharp mind, and a wicked sense of humour – one particular little joke that he has perpetrated upon his owner on several occasions being to exit the dressage arena well before the end of his test.

However, he loves jumping, particularly cross-country, and while he hasn't the quality or speed to make an eventer, or the scope to become an affiliated showjumper, he would make a splendid hunter, a job that I am certain he would relish. I have suggested to his owner that she sell him for this purpose, but she won't hear of it, yet will not take up hunting. So, she is stuck with a horse who does his best to avoid dressage, while this is her chosen pursuit! Who is being unfair to whom, I wonder?

produced a sound like a gunshot as they parted company with the tooth. To my astonishment, as they lay in his hand, the points were triangles probably 1.5cm (1/2in) high and 2cm (3/4in) in length. No wonder the poor animal had been so unhappy in his mouth. Needless to say, he was a different horse within a few days.

Many horses who buck or rear are doing so through pain – often in the back – or the fear of pain that has gone before. Most horses who are bucking through pain will stop doing so once the site of the pain is treated, unless the habit has become ingrained, when it is best for the less experienced rider to send the horse to an expert to be rehabilitated.

THE BEST TEACHER OF ALL

One of my best schoolmasters, Butch, had been a chronic rearer, to the point of going over backwards. We acquired him just as he was about to be destroyed, aged eight, because he was deemed dangerous to ride. His owner/breeders were two ladies in their late fifties, who had bred him to race. He broke down in training at five and had then been sent to an event yard, as he was by a stallion that had been a prolific sire of event horses. It transpired that he had fallen, and had obviously damaged his pelvis. His rider had not realized that this was the case, and had beaten him into continuing to jump. Very shortly afterwards, he began to rear as soon as he was pointed at a fence. Not long after that, he learned to throw himself over backwards. He was sent back to his owners as being too dangerous. They had his back checked, and it was found that his pelvis was misaligned. After treatment, he still expected to be in pain when ridden, and would rear when hacking out alone and if taken anywhere near a jump.

I heard about him just in time. Butch's owners loved him dearly, but were retiring from breeding and closing their stud, and could no longer keep him. Rather than have him end up in the wrong home, responsibly – but very reluctantly – they had decided to have him put down. I got in touch and pleaded with them to come and meet us and see if they liked our yard and the way our horses were treated. They

Butch, 24-years-old and now retired, with Shifty, my Jack Russell, and me posing for an article devoted to him in *Horse* magazine

came, liked what they saw, and Butch – now 24 years old and about to be retired except for light hacking – has been a great friend ever since.

I gave him time to settle in, riding him only on the flat and hacking out in company. Within a few weeks he began to trust me and, realizing that I was not going to inflict any pain on him, started to pop over small jumps in the indoor school. However, hacking out alone was still a major problem. He would nap and rear at junctions if he did not want to go in the direction I did. Instead of insisting that he go where I chose, when he stopped and refused to move, I sat still and said, 'Well chum, if you've got half an hour to waste, so have I.' Before I set out for each ride, I informed my yard staff where I intended to go, just in case my ploy did not work out as I hoped!

After about five minutes, Butch would start to wonder why we were standing still and going nowhere. I would then ask him, very gently, to go forwards. If he still refused, we would stand there again, me remaining totally passive in the saddle, until he showed signs of wanting to move. Within a few weeks, I could ride him anywhere. Because I did not pick a fight with him, but instead outwitted him, he became bored with the idea of resisting and found that life was really rather more fun if he went along with me. He has never reared again in nearly 17 years of partnership, and after retraining in the Classical way, he has taught dozens of students to ride with lightness, as an exemplary schoolmaster. I was able to compete on him in showjumping and to event him again at riding club level. He has been the lunge horse *par excellence*, also carrying me sidesaddle with great pride, and is now due for honourable retirement.

Butch does not owe me a penny – and to think that if a friend had not told me about him, so long ago, he would have been dead for 17 years. People have said to me what a lucky horse he was. I always reply that no, it is me who has been the lucky one. It was he who first made me realize that there had to be another way of training, without the force that I knew, had I tried to use it, would get me deeper into trouble with him. It was through him that I came to learn the best, most humane Classical methods. It was he who gave me the motivation to write articles, and subsequently this book, to spread the word that 'Enlightened Equitation' should be the goal of all who profess to love the horse.

ACKNOWLEDGEMENTS

I would like to thank my friends, Alan and Margaret Cox, for their unfailing support and encouragement, and their help in so many ways. I have watched the best-known trainers in the world and I have still to find one that could match Margaret's wonderfully clear, concise, analytical teaching, which has greatly helped to clarify and consolidate my own knowledge of the training of the horse.

My thanks also to Captain Desi Lorent. Desi taught me the lightness and finesse that is the prerogative of the Classically trained rider. Without his help, I would never have been able to refine my own teaching of the rider, particularly my understanding of the remedial work for which I am perhaps best known.

For help with this book, I offer my thanks to my good friend Julian Marczak A.B.R.S. (Prin. Dip.) (T.C.), L.G.S.M., L.C.G.I., chief instructor and co-proprietor of Suzanne's Riding School, Harrow Weald, Middlesex, for allowing me to use photographs of Emperador and Doric. I would like to congratulate Suzanne's on their sixtieth anniversary this year, 1999, making the school the longest established in the country. Julian trained as a Classical musician at the Guildhall School of Music and Drama, before joining his mother, Suzanne, in running the school. He trained as a Classical rider with Charles Harris, Daniel Pevsner and the great Nuño Oliveira. Julian feels that his musical training has greatly enhanced his understanding and appreciation of riding as an Art. As a lifelong musician and semi-professional watercolour artist, I would totally agree.

My thanks to my pupils, for being such interesting demonstration models, to photographer Iain Burns, whose sense of humour and skill always make him a pleasure to work with, and to artist Dianne Breeze, for her superb illustrations.

Last but by no means least, I offer my gratitude to my other great friends Jonathan and Anne Broughton-Heyes, for Jon's magnificent invention the Equisimulator, which has enabled me to revolutionise my teaching, and for all their help through the last few years. I have been fortunate indeed to have such friends and teachers, to whom Fate has led me, at times when I needed them most.

INDEX